AQA Religious Studies A

Islam

GCSE

Diana Hayden

Series editor

Cynthia Bartlett

OXFORD

UNIVERSITY PRESS

G000279188

OXFORD
UNIVERSITY PRESS

Great Clarendon Street, Oxford, OX2 6DP, United Kingdom

Oxford University Press is a department of the University of Oxford.
It furthers the University's objective of excellence in research, scholarship,
and education by publishing worldwide. Oxford is a registered trade mark of
Oxford University Press in the UK and in certain other countries

British Library Cataloguing in Publication Data
Data available

978-1-4085-0476-5

3

MIX
Paper from
responsible sources
FSC
www.fsc.org   FSC® C007785

Printed in Great Britain by Bell & Bain Ltd, Glasgow

Acknowledgements

Cover photograph: Sean Sprague/Still Pictures
Illustrations: Rupert Besley, Paul McCaffrey (c/o Sylvie Poggio Artists Agency), Pantek Arts Ltd and Dave Russell Illustration
Page make-up: Pantek Arts Ltd, Maidstone

The authors and publishers wish to thank the following for permission to use copyright material:

1.6A Extract from *The Islamic World: Past and Present*, John L. Esposito (ed.), OUP (2004). Reprinted with permission of Oxford University Press UK; 1.7A Extract adapted from *Islam the Natural Way*, A. Hamid, MELS (1989). Reprinted with permission of the publishers; 1.12A Quoted from page 153 of *Islam: Beliefs and Teachings* (8th edition), Ghulam Sarwar, Muslim Educational Trust (reprinted 2008); 1.12B Quoted from *Introducing Islam*, © Ziauddin Sardar, Icon Books (1994); 2.2A © SCM Press, an imprint of Hymns Ancient & Modern Ltd. Used by permission; 2.2A Extracts from 'Let us be Muslims', S. Mawdudi, Islamic Foundation (1982). Reprinted with permission; 2.4A Extracts from 'Let us be Muslims' by S. Mawdudi, Islamic Foundation (1982) Reprinted with permission; 2.9A Extract from *The Autobiography of Malcolm X*, Malcolm X and Alex Haley, Hutchinson and Random House Inc. © 1964 Alex Haley and Malcolm X. © 1965 Alex Haley and Betty Shabazz. Reprinted by permission of The Random House Group Limited UK and Random House, Inc USA; 3.8A Extract from www.yourfamily.org.uk. Reprinted with kind permission of The NSPCC and the family; 3.10A Extract from *Sacrifice*, Khurram Murad, Islamic Foundation (1985). Reprinted with permission; 4.7A Extract from *The Islamic attitude to social relations in the light of Sura al-hujurat verses 10-12*, Muhammad Manazir Ahsan, Islamic Foundation (1979). Reprinted with permission; 4.8A Extract adapted from *Islam the Natural Way*, A. Hamid, MELS (1989). Reprinted with permission of the publishers; 6.4A Independent News and Media (2008); 6.5A Extract adapted from Islam the Natural Way, A. Hamid, MELS (1989). Reprinted with permission of the publishers; 6.5B Extract from *The Trouble with Islam Today*, Manji Irshad, Mainstream Publishing Company (2004). Reprinted with permission; 6.8B extracts from *The Holy Qur'an: English Translation and Commentary*, Abdullah Yusuf Ali. Reprinted with permission of IPCI-Islamic Vision.

Photographs

Ahmed Saad: 3.5D; **Alamy:** 4.5C,5.2B; **Art Directors:** 1.2D, 3.3B, 3.3C, 3.5C, 6.8A; **Corbis:** 1.9A, 2.8B, 3.4A, 3.4C, 3.8A; **Fotolia:** CO1, 1.1B, 1.1C, 1.2B, 1.2C, 1.3A, 1.3E, 1.4A, 1.5A, 1.7C, 1.8A, 1.8C, 1.9B, 1.10C, 1.12A, 1.13A, 1.13C, 2.1C, 2.1D, 2.1E, 2.1G, 2.2A, 2.3B, 2.3D, 2.4A, 2.4B, 2.4C, 2.5A, 2.5B, 2.5C, 2.6B, 2.6C, 2.9D, CC2, CO3, 3.1D, 3.1E, 3.1G, 3.4B, 3.8C, 3.11A, CO4, 4.1A, 4.1B, 4.1C, 4.2D, 4.3C, 4.4C, 4.5A, 4.5D, 4.7D, 4.8A, 4.8C, 4.9B, 4.9C, 4.9D, 5.2A, 5.5A, 5.5B, 5.6A, 5.9A, 5.9C, 5.9D, 5.9E, 6.1A, 6.2A, 6.2B, 6.2C, 6.3A, 6.3C, 6.3D, 6.4B, 6.4D, 6.5B, 6.5D, 6.6A, 6.6B, 6.7B, 6.9A; **Getty:** 1.1A, 1.6A, 1.6C, 1.13B, 2.1F, 2.8C, 2.8D, 2.9B, 3.6C, 3.10A, 3.10B, 4.3D, 4.6A, 4.7A, 4.7B, 4.7F, 4.8A, CO5, 5.2E, 5.3B, 5.9B, CO6, 6.6C, 6.6D, 6.7A, 6.8B; **iStockphoto:** 1.1D, 1.2A, 1.2E, 1.3B, 1.3D, 1.3F, 1.4B, 1.5B, 1.5C, 1.6D, 1.7A, 1.8B, 1.11A, 1.11B, 1.12B, 1.12C, CO2, 2.3C, 2.4D, 2.6A, 2.7A, 2.7C, 2.9A, 2.9B, 2.10A, 2.10B, 2.10C, 3.1A, 3.1B, 3.1C, 3.2A, 3.2B, 3.2C, 3.2D, 3.3D, 3.3E, 3.3F, 3.5A, 3.5B, 3.6A, 3.7A, 3.7B, 3.7C, 3.7D, 3.8B, 3.8D, 3.9A, 3.9B, 3.9C, 3.10C, 4.1D, 4.2A, 4.2B, 4.2C, 4.3B, 4.4A, 4.4B, 4.5B, 4.6B, 4.6C, 4.7C, 4.9A, 5.2C, 5.3A, 5.4B, 5.5C, 5.6B, 5.7B, 5.8A, 5.8B, 5.8C, 5.8D, 6.1A, 6.1C, 6.3B, 6.5C, 6.6E, 6.9B, 6.9C; **Photographers Direct:** 2.2B World Religions Photo Library/Christine Osbourne, 2.7B World Religions Photo Library/Camerapix, 2.7D World Religions Photo Library/Camerapix, 4.3A Alex Segre, 5.1A Rosina Redwood Photography, 5.1B World Religions Photo Library/Paul Gapper, 5.2D World Religions Photo Library/Jill Brown, 5.4A World Religions Photo Library/Camerapix; **Photolibrary:** 5.7D; **Photoshot:** 1.6b; **Rex Features:** 1.7b, 3.3a.

Although we have made every effort to trace and contact all
copyright holders before publication this has not been possible in all
cases. If notified, the publisher will rectify any errors or omissions at
the earliest opportunity.

Links to third party websites are provided by Oxford in good faith
and for information only. Oxford disclaims any responsibility for
the materials contained in any third party website referenced in
this work.

Contents

The publisher has worked to make sure that this book offers you the best possible support for your GCSE course. You can be sure that it gives you useful support when you are preparing for your exams.

■ How to use this book

Learning Objectives

At the beginning of each section or topic you'll find a list of Learning Objectives based on the requirements of the specification.

Objectives

Objectives

Objectives

Objectives

First objective.

Second objective.

Study Tips

Don't forget to look at the Study tips throughout the book to help you with your study and prepare for your exam.

Study tip

Don't forget to look at the Study tips throughout the book to help you with your study and prepare for your exam.

Practice Questions

These offer opportunities to practise doing questions in the style that you can expect in your exam so that you can be fully prepared on the day.

Practice questions are reproduced by permission of the Assessment and Qualifications Alliance.

GCSE Islam

This book is written specifically for GCSE students studying the AQA Religious Studies Specification A, *Unit 8 Islam*. You will be studying six different topics and the Muslim beliefs and teachings that relate to each of these topics. Many of these teachings are from the Qur'an as it is the main written authority in Islam. You do not have to be a Muslim to be successful but an interest in Religious Studies and a willingness to find out more will help you.

Following this unit alone will earn you a GCSE short course qualification in Religious Studies. If you combine it with another unit, you will be eligible for a full course GCSE in Religious Studies. In order to qualify for a grade you will have to sit one 90-minute examination for each unit you study, i.e. for short course one examination, and for full course two examinations. This is the only form of final assessment.

■ Topics in this unit

In the examination, you will be asked to answer questions based on the following six topics:

Beliefs and sources of authority

In this topic you will study the key beliefs about God, prophets, life after death, and the two main sources of authority in Islam: the Qur'an and the hadith. You will also study the life and work of the Prophet Muhammad.

The Five Pillars of Islam

These are the five main duties of Islam. You will study how they are put into practice, their meaning and their importance.

Worship

In this topic you will study the mosque, its design and how it is used. You will also consider the festivals of Eid ul Fitr and Eid ul Adha.

Personal lifestyle

This topic includes Muslim attitudes to food, alcohol and dress, and the character of the Muslim community. You will consider how Muslim life reflects the core beliefs of Islam.

Family life

In this topic you will study Muslim attitudes to marriage, including arranged marriages, polygamy and divorce. You will also consider such issues as sexual relationships outside marriage, attitudes to homosexuality, family life and worship in the home.

Justice and equality

In this topic you will study Muslim views on equality, prejudice and discrimination, and the role and status of women in Islam.

■ Assessment guidance

Your examination will be in two parts. Part A will have four questions split into shorter parts. You have to answer all of the questions in Part A which will total 48 marks.

Part B will contain two questions. Again, they will be split into smaller parts. You are required to answer just one of these, so you will have to choose which one. Each question carries 24 marks so they are longer than in Part A and it is likely that you will have to give some more detailed answers.

Every chapter in this book finishes with assessment guidance, using practice questions. There is also a summary of what you have learnt in the chapter, together with a sample answer for you to mark yourself. Use the large grid opposite to help you to do this.

Examination questions will test two assessment objectives

AO1	Describe, explain and analyse, using knowledge and understanding.	50%
AO2	Use evidence and reasoned argument to express and evaluate personal responses, informed insights and differing viewpoints.	50%

The exam will also take into account the quality of your written communication – how clearly you express yourself and how well you communicate your meaning. The grid below also gives you some guidance on the sort of quality expected at different levels.

Levels of response mark scheme

Levels	Criteria for AO1	Criteria for AO2	Quality of written communication	Marks
0	Nothing relevant or worthy of credit	An unsupported opinion or no relevant evaluation	The candidate's presentation, spelling, punctuation and grammar seriously obstruct understanding	0 marks
Level 1	Something relevant or worthy of credit	An opinion supported by simple reason	The candidate presents some relevant information in a simple form. The text produced is usually legible. Spelling, punctuation and grammar allow meaning to be derived, although errors are sometimes obstructive	1 mark
Level 2	Elementary knowledge and understanding, e.g. two simple points	An opinion supported by one developed reason or two simple reasons		2 marks
Level 3	Sound knowledge and understanding	An opinion supported by one well developed reason or several simple reasons. **N.B. Candidates who make no religious comment should not achieve more than Level 3**	The candidate presents relevant information in a way which assists with the communication of meaning. The text produced is legible. Spelling, punctuation and grammar are sufficiently accurate not to obscure meaning	3 marks
Level 4	A clear knowledge and understanding with some development	An opinion supported by two developed reasons with reference to religion		4 marks
Level 5	A detailed answer with some analysis, as appropriate	Evidence of reasoned consideration of two different points of view, showing informed insights and knowledge and understanding of religion	The candidate presents relevant information coherently, employing structure and style to render meaning clear. The text produced is legible. Spelling, punctuation and grammar are sufficiently accurate to render meaning clear	5 marks
Level 6	A full and coherent answer showing good analysis, as appropriate	A well-argued response, with evidence of reasoned consideration of two different points of view showing informed insights and ability to apply knowledge and understanding of religion effectively		6 marks

Please note that mark schemes change over time. Please refer to the AQA website for the very latest information.

Note: In evaluation answers to questions worth only 3 marks, the first three levels apply. Questions which are marked out of 3 marks do not ask for two views, but reasons for your own opinion.

Successful study of this unit will result in a Short Course GCSE award. Study of one further unit will provide a Full Course GCSE award. Other units in Specification A which may be taken to achieve a Full Course GCSE award are:

- Unit 1 Christianity
- Unit 2 Christianity: Ethics
- Unit 3 Roman Catholicism
- Unit 4 Roman Catholicism: Ethics
- Unit 5 St Mark's Gospel
- Unit 6 St Luke's Gospel
- Unit 7 Philosophy of Religion
- Unit 9 Islam: Ethics
- Unit 10 Judaism
- Unit 11 Judaism: Ethics
- Unit 12 Buddhism
- Unit 13 Hinduism
- Unit 14 Sikhism

1.1 Introduction to Islam

■ Islam

According to its followers, **Islam** is the final version of God's religion. It was first revealed to Adam, the first man, and finally revealed to a man named Muhammad who was born in what is now Saudi Arabia around 1400 years ago. Islam is an Arabic word which means 'surrender', 'obedience' or 'submission'. **Muslims** believe that they should surrender to the will of God. The word also means 'peace'. This is because Muslims believe that if a person totally obeys the will of **Allah**, they will achieve peace in themselves.

Beliefs and teachings

The religion with God is Islam.

Qur'an 3:19

You who believe, obey God and the Messenger.

Qur'an 4:59

Who can be better in religion than he who submits his whole self to God?

Qur'an 4:125

Tawhid

One of the key beliefs of Islam is the belief that there is only one God. This is called the doctrine of **tawhid**. It is seen in the Arabic word Muslims use for God, the word Allah which means the one and only God.

Beliefs and teachings

Say: He is Allah, the One and only!
Allah, the eternal absolute!
He is the father of none, and none is his father.
And there is none like unto him.

Qur'an 112

Allah. There is no god but he, the Living, the Self-subsisting, Eternal. No slumber can seize him nor sleep. His are all things in the heavens and on earth.

Qur'an 2:255

Muslims believe that God is the one and only creator and controller of everything and that nothing, good or bad, can happen unless God allows it to.

Muslims have a duty to accept whatever happens as the will of God. This means that however bad it appears, they must believe that God has allowed it to happen for a good reason. This is why Muslims add the words 'God willing' (inshallah) when they promise to do

Objectives

Understand the terms Islam, Muslim, Allah and tawhid.

Key terms

Islam: the name of the religion followed by Muslims; to surrender to the will of God; peace.

Muslim: one who has submitted to the will of Allah and has accepted Islam.

Allah: the Islamic name for God.

Tawhid: oneness and unity of Allah.

⃝⃝ links

For an introduction to the early life of Muhammad, see pages 22–23.

A *Muslims believe that Allah is the one and only God*

B *The results of an earthquake*

Beliefs and teachings

No disaster strikes except with God's permission.

Qur'an 64:11

Discussion activity

Why can no one be certain that they will be able to keep their promises? Discuss this with a partner or in a small group.

C *The word Allah*

something. They are showing their belief that they are not in control of what happens and that they will only be able to keep their promise, or carry out their plan, if God allows them to. Some Muslims believe that this means that God controls everything we do and that we have no free will of our own. Others believe that God has allowed us free will. This means that he does not make us do anything but he allows us to choose how to behave.

Only God should be worshipped

It is not enough for Muslims to believe that there is only one God. They must also show this in the way they live their lives. Islam teaches that there is nothing that shares God's role or importance; He has no partner or son, so only God should be worshipped. To show this in everyday life Muslims must never make anything more important than God and must serve God alone. This is what the word Muslim means: 'one who has submitted to God'. In the life of a Muslim, God must always come first.

Extension activity

Beliefs can affect both actions and attitudes. How might the belief that God controls everything affect the attitude Muslims have to life?

Activities

1 Learn the meaning of these important words: Islam, Muslim, Allah and tawhid. Write the meanings in your book then close the book and see if you can remember the meanings.

2 Explain why Muslims add the words 'God willing' when they make any promises.

3 What does Islam teach about the bad things that happen in life?

D *Islam means peace*

Summary

You should now understand the terms Islam, Muslim, Allah and tawhid. Islam is the way of peace and submission to God; tawhid is the belief that there is only one God.

Study tip

You should learn the meaning of all the key terms given in this book.

The nature of God

God is unique

Islam teaches that God is unique; there is nothing like Him. God cannot be described or pictured because there is nothing like God that we can imagine or compare Him to. For that reason there are no images or pictures of God in Muslim books or homes, or in a mosque, the Muslim place of worship. Mosques are often decorated with script from the Qur'an instead.

Objectives

Understand Muslim beliefs about the nature of God.

∞ links

To find out more about the mosque, see Chapter 3, page 58.

To learn more about the Qur'an, see pages 16–19.

Beliefs and teachings

This is Allah, Your Lord! There is no God but he, the creator of all things. Worship him, he has the power over all things. No vision can grasp him, but his grasp is over all things; he is above all understanding, yet he is aware of all things.

Qur'an 6:102–103

A *Muslim places of worship are decorated with Arabic script, not images*

B *The Arabic words on this flag are Allahu Akbar, God is the greatest*

God is beyond human understanding

God is so great that he is beyond human understanding. Muslims hear and repeat the words 'Allahu Akbar' many times a day. They mean 'God is the greatest' and they remind Muslims that God is greater than anything they can possibly imagine. We can see what this means when we try to imagine where God is. Everything around us is in one place at a time, but God is said to be beyond everywhere. According to Islam, He is both immanent and transcendent. Immanent means within everything, transcendent means beyond everything, and God is both. In our limited human thinking this does not really make sense. However, Islam teaches that when Muslims hear the names that God has given himself, God helps them to understand his nature.

■ The names of God

According to tradition, there are 99 Names of God and Muslims have searched the Qur'an and hadith to find them. Many Muslims will memorise the Names and recite them in their private prayers. Each name helps them to feel the presence of God. Many of the Names remind Muslims of God's greatness, power and authority; others show his care and concern for human beings.

> *Names of God: The All-powerful; The All-seeing; The Provider; The Kind One.*

Activity

Here are three Names of God. Think about the meaning of each one.

- God is The All-Aware
- God is The Judge
- God is The Guardian

Each Name should remind Muslims that God is with them. If you knew that God was watching you now, judging you now, and guarding you now, what might it feel like?

God is The Merciful and The Compassionate

God's character is summed up in these words which are repeated by Muslims 17 times a day in their daily prayers. The words remind them that God cares for them and has provided everything they need. He understands their suffering and their weaknesses, and forgives those who truly regret what they have done. These are qualities Muslims are expected to show in their own lives.

Muslims dedicate everything they are doing to God by saying the words 'In the name of God The Merciful and The Compassionate' before they start. This phrase is known as the Bismillah. By using it, Muslims show that they are always serving God by carrying out his commands.

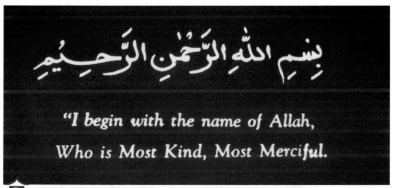

بِسْمِ اللهِ الرَّحْمٰنِ الرَّحِيْمِ

"I begin with the name of Allah, Who is Most Kind, Most Merciful.

D *All new projects, like writing a book, should be dedicated to God*

Summary

You should now understand Muslim beliefs about the nature of God. God is beyond human understanding, but he makes himself known in ways we can partly understand.

Beliefs and teachings

Allah's are the most beautiful names; call on him thereby.

Qur'an 7:180

Extension activity

Look up the 99 Names of God on a website such as www.jannah.org/articles/names.html

What do these names show about Muslim ideas about God?

C *Prayer beads are used to help recitation of the Names of God*

Study tip

In the examination you may need to be able to link beliefs with the actions or attitudes they lead to.

∞ links

See the Glossary for a definition of the term 'Bismillah'.

E *Elderly man reciting the names of Allah*

Risalah is the teaching about **prophethood**, which is the channel of communication between God and human beings. Muslims believe that Islam was revealed to the first of the prophets, Adam, at the beginning of time and was therefore the first religion. When human beings lost, forgot, misunderstood or even deliberately changed that message, God sent other prophets to remind them and call them back to the true path. This continued until Muhammad, the last of the prophets, was chosen by God.

Objectives

Know and understand the Muslim beliefs about risalah and consider their importance.

Key terms

Risalah: prophethood; channel of communication.

Prophethood: channel of communication with God (risalah).

The Prophet: title often used for Muhammad, the last of the prophets.

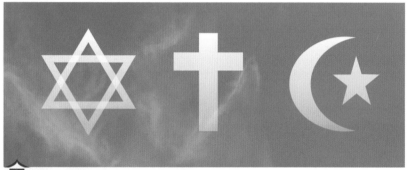

A   *The symbols of Judaism, Christianity and Islam*

Prophets

Prophets are human beings chosen by God to carry out a special role as his messengers. The Qur'an names 25 of them but according to Muslim tradition there have been 124,000 prophets. The most important prophets are called Messengers. These include Moses, the prophet of the Jews, and Jesus, the prophet of the Christians, as well as Muhammad, **the Prophet** of Islam. They each received a book from God: Moses received the Torah; Jesus the Gospel; and Muhammad the Qur'an.

B   *Arabic text meaning 'Muhammad the Prophet', from inside a mosque in Cairo*

Adam	Job	Enoch
Moses	Noah	Aaron
Hud	Ezekiel	Salib
David	Abraham	Solomon
Ishmael	Elijah	Isaac
Elisha	Lot	Jonah
Jacob	Zachari'ah	Joseph
John	Shuaib	Jesus
	Muhammad	

C   *The 25 prophets named in the Qur'an*

Muslims believe that each prophet brought the same religion and perfectly carried out the role God had given him. Each one also led a good life which set an example to others of how God wanted people to live. Muslims are commanded to believe the message that was sent down to these earlier prophets, to follow their example, and to treat all of them with respect. For that reason, when they mention a prophet's name they call for God's blessing on him. In English, this is often written as 'pbuh', meaning 'peace be upon him'.

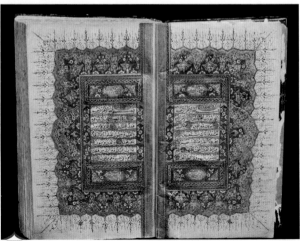

D   *An old copy of the Qur'an, which is a record of the message sent to Prophet Muhammed*

Say: 'We believe in Allah, and the revelation given to us, and to Abraham, Ishmael, Isaac, Jacob, and the Tribes, and that given to Moses and Jesus, and that given to all prophets from their Lord. We make no difference between one and another of them.'

Qur'an 2:136

Research activity

Choose one of the prophets before Muhammad and find out what the Qur'an says about their life and message.

Islam teaches that the message brought by the earlier prophets was not recorded properly. Only the Qur'an is seen as an accurate record of God's message. Muslims believe that each of the earlier messages was passed on perfectly by the prophets but partly forgotten, misunderstood or distorted by those who heard it before it was written down. That means, for example, that the Bible is believed to be an unreliable record of God's word in which serious misunderstandings of God's message have been recorded.

Angels

The word of God is brought to the Messengers by angels. Angels are supernatural beings, created by God out of light. They are sinless, so they are able to receive God's words directly from him and pass these on to the prophets. Angels also take information from humans and present it to God. These are the recording angels who write down everything each person thinks, says or does. This record is kept in a book and is presented as evidence, in front of God, at the final judgement.

Activities

1 Explain what Muslims understand by the word prophet.
2 Name the first and the last prophet of God according to Islam.
3 Name the Holy Books brought by the prophets Jesus and Muhammad.
4 How did the prophets receive their message from God?
5 Why are the prophets still important in Islam today?

Beliefs and teachings

God sent prophets as bearers of good news and as warners and revealed to them the book with the truth.

Qur'an 2:153

Summary

You should now know and understand the Muslim beliefs about risalah, and be able to discuss their importance. God has sent prophets throughout human history, and Muhammad, the Prophet, is believed by Muslims to be the last of God's prophets.

You would be able to explain or develop your answer to any question about risalah by referring to any of the prophets of Islam.

E   *Muslims believe the Bible has not recorded God's words accurately*

F   *Angels are beings of light*

⚭ links

Read more about the role of angels in the account of Muhammad's first revelation experience on page 24.

Akhirah

According to Islam, death is not the end. It is the beginning of a new stage in life, the stage of akhirah, the afterlife. The present life is a preparation for **akhirah**. The Qur'an and Muslim traditions describe the events after death very vividly.

Life after death

Many Muslims believe that when the body dies the person will continue to live. They will feel themselves being prepared for burial and being put in the grave. Then they will hear the last footsteps walking away from the grave. Then they will wait until the **Day of Judgement**. This state of waiting after death is called barzakh, which means 'a barrier': people cannot come back across the barrier to put things right or to warn those still living. See the Qur'an 23:99–100.

Muslims believe that as they lie in the grave they will be questioned about their faith by two angels. Those who answer correctly will be shown the reward that will be theirs, whereas those who have denied God will be shown the punishments to come. Some believe that these punishments will actually start in the grave. Others believe that people will sleep in their graves until the end of the world, when the Day of Judgement will come.

Last day and judgement

Muslims believe that when the universe has completed the purpose for which God made it, He will end it. Only God knows when this will be. The angel Israfil will blow a trumpet to announce the last day and the world as we know it will be destroyed. The dead will be resurrected. This means that they will be raised back to life by God. The Qur'an suggests that they will be given new and different bodies. Everyone who has ever lived will be called in front of God for judgement and the book of their life will be given to them, for them to read out. At that moment, humans will celebrate all the good they have done and face up to all the evil they have done. If the book is given to them in their right hand they will go to heaven; if they get it in their left hand they will go to hell.

Paradise and hell

Paradise, or heaven, is the reward for faith and good works. The Qur'an includes many descriptions of both paradise and hell. Paradise is described as gardens of happiness.

Beliefs and teachings

They will be on thrones encrusted with gold and precious stones
Leaning on them, facing each other
Youths will serve them
With goblets, beakers, and cups filled with clear-flowing fountains
No after effects will they receive from these, nor will they be intoxicated
And with any fruits that they may choose
And the flesh of fowl that they may want
And there will be companions with beautiful eyes
Like pearls. Rewards for the deeds of their past life.

Qur'an 56:15–22

Objectives

Understand beliefs about akhirah and consider their importance.

Key terms

Akhirah: everlasting life after death.

Day of Judgement: the day when Allah will decide about individual deeds, good and bad, and on reward and punishment.

Paradise: place of perfect happiness; the afterlife.

Hell: eternal separation from Allah.

∞ links

See the Glossary for a definition of the term 'barzakh'.

A *A Muslim graveyard. Some Muslims believe that people are being rewarded or punished in the grave*

Extension activity

Find out more about events following death from these hadith: Bukhari 2:400; 2:422; 2:461

Visit the website www.sacred-texts.com and follow the links to Islam, Hadith of Bukhari, and Volume Two. You will then find direct links to the hadith referenced in this activity.

Hell is the punishment for rejecting God and doing evil. Hell is described as a place of fire, of great torment.

Beliefs and teachings

They will be in the midst of fire and in boiling water
And in the shades of black smoke
Nothing will be there to refresh or to please.

Qur'an 56:42–44

But those who deny their Lord there will be clothes of Fire: over their heads will be poured out boiling water which will scald what is in their bodies, as well as their skins. Every time they wish to get away from anguish, they will be forced back in.

Qur'an 22:19–21

Every Muslim accepts the word of God in the Qur'an but there are different opinions about what these verses mean. Some believe that they describe exactly what heaven and hell will be like. Many believe that they are only suggesting the wonders of heaven and the horrors of hell because these are actually beyond human understanding. Many believe that these are symbolic descriptions of a more spiritual existence because there will be no physical existence of the kind that has existed on earth.

B   *The hell of fire*

■ The importance of the belief in an afterlife

Life after death guarantees that people will be rewarded or punished for everything they do, so it makes life fair. The hope of paradise encourages people to do good; the threat of hell encourages them to avoid doing evil. Muslims believe that life is worthwhile, no matter how difficult or painful it is, because it leads to something better. All this makes the belief in life after death one of the most important beliefs in Islam.

Summary

You should now understand Muslim beliefs about akhirah and be aware of how these beliefs have a strong influence on the way Muslims live their lives.

Activities

1   Is it reasonable to believe in life after death?

2   How may people's lives be affected by what they believe about life after death?

3   'Muslims only obey God because they are frightened of hell.' Do you agree? Give reasons for your answer, showing that you have thought about more than one point of view.

4   'A God who punishes people is not compassionate.' What do you think? Explain your opinion.

Study tip

It is important for you to know what Muslims believe about life after death as well as to form an opinion of your own, with arguments to support it.

Activity

5   Create three revision cards. On one card draw a picture of a grave, on another paradise, on a third hell fire. Write on the back of each card a brief description of what Muslims believe will happen in each of these places. Use these later to test yourself.

Revelation of the Qur'an

The **Qur'an** is the holy book of Islam which Muslims believe was revealed to Muhammad, the last prophet of Islam. The Qur'an was delivered bit by bit during the 23 years of Muhammad's career, from the time of his call to be a prophet in 610 CE, to about 80 days before his death in 632 CE. Muslims believe that God does not speak directly to human beings because he is so much greater than we are, and that the Qur'an was revealed to Muhammad by the Angel Jibril (Gabriel in English).

The experiences of the **revelation** of God's word were so strong that Muhammad sometimes found them hard to bear. He would sometimes sweat and shake when the messages came to him. He described some of his experiences in a hadith:

Beliefs and teachings

Sometimes it is like the ringing of a bell, this form of inspiration is the hardest of all and it passes off after I have grasped what is inspired. Sometimes the Angel comes in the form of a man and talks to me and I grasp whatever he says.

Hadith

Many of the verses revealed answered questions asked by Muhammad or by the people, or they solved difficulties the people were facing. Some were very short; others were quite long and detailed.

A *The revelation of the Qur'an is often described as the coming of a holy light*

Research activity 🔍

Find out more about the Muslim idea of inspiration. You may find it useful in your research to input the word 'wahy' into an internet search engine.

Objectives

Know and understand Muslim accounts of the revelation and compilation of the Qur'an.

Key terms

Qur'an: the Holy Book revealed to the Prophet Muhammad by the angel Jibril. Allah's final revelation to humankind.

Revelation: the words of the Qur'an being shown to Muhammad; Allah shows himself to believers.

Compilation: a gathering together into one book of material from more than one source.

Surah: a division of the Qur'an. There are 114 in all.

∞ links

You will find an account of the first revelation received by Muhammad on page 24.

Beliefs and teachings

It is not fitting for a man that Allah should speak to him except by inspiration, or from behind a veil, or by the sending of a messenger to reveal, with Allah's permission, what Allah wills: for He is Most High, Most Wise. And so have We, by Our command, sent inspiration to you (Muhammad). You did not know before what was Revelation, and what was Faith; but We have made the Qur'an a Light to guide men; and truly you guide men to the Straight Way – The way of God.

Qur'an 42:51–53

■ Compilation of the Qur'an

According to Muslim tradition, after Muhammad recited the revelations his followers memorised them or wrote them down on anything they could find. When he died, the words of the Qur'an were found on scraps of bone, leather and parchment, and in the memories of men. The first collection, or **compilation**, of this material was made in Madinah just after the Prophet's death. In other parts of the Muslim world, Muslim preachers were reciting the Qur'an from memory. In 650 CE, Caliph Uthman decided that one official written version of the Qur'an was needed because some of the preachers were not remembering the Qur'an correctly. Today all copies of the Arabic Qur'an are based on Uthman's version.

For easy reference the revelations were divided into 114 **surahs**, or chapters, and these were divided into verses. The first surah contained the words recited in each daily prayer, after that the surahs were arranged from longest to shortest. This means that the material does not appear in the Qur'an in the order in which it was revealed.

B *All the earliest copies of the Qur'an were handwritten*

Activities

1 How long did the revelation of the Qur'an take?
2 What happened to the Prophet when he was receiving a revelation?
3 What were the verses of the Qur'an first written on?
4 Why did Uthman decide an official written version of the Qur'an was needed?
5 What is a surah?
6 How many surahs are there in the Qur'an? What order were they put in?

C *The first verse of the Holy Qur'an, surrounded by Islamic cultural drawing*

Extension activity

You can carry out this task with a partner, and then present your conclusions to the rest of your class.

Some people do not believe that Muhammad was visited by an Angel or received the Qur'an from God. What reasons could they give for their belief? Are these good reasons?

Summary

You should now know and understand Muslim accounts of the revelation and compilation of the Qur'an. The Qur'an was revealed by Jibril a little at a time over 23 years. An official version of the Qur'an was completed in 650 CE.

Study tip

You should be able to answer each of the activity questions from memory by the time you are ready for the examination.

1.6 The Qur'an (2)

◼ Recitation of the Qur'an

When Muhammad received his first revelation, he was commanded to recite the words that came to him. He then taught them to others who also memorised and recited them. In this way everyone could hear God speaking directly to them, through the voices of others. This continues today. Qur'an recitation is one of the most important duties for Muslims. This is because when they do this they are passing on God's words, on God's behalf, to those who have not yet heard them. **Recitation** is an art form. Every phrase should be delivered perfectly to honour their author. Some Muslims have learned the Qur'an by heart in Arabic and the person who can do so is called a hafiz.

Research activity 🔍

1 You can listen to the Qur'an being recited on many websites. Remember as you listen that for a Muslim these are the actual words of God.

Case study

Reciting the Qur'an

The public reading of the Qur'an is a major form of performance art in the Islamic world. Crowds fill stadiums to hear musical and poetic recitations. Listeners derive great pleasure from the rich rhyming prose of the Qur'an. Muslims hire reciters for weddings, funerals, conferences and a variety of other events. The most famous reciters can earn a comfortable living from their performances and commercial recordings. Many countries hold Qur'an recitation contests which attract large audiences. Both children and adults compete at local, regional, and national events. Winners receive trophies and other rewards.

www.oxfordislamicstudies.com

A *A public reading of the Qur'an*

Activity

1 Read the case study 'Reciting the Qur'an' and use this and other information on this page to answer the following questions.

a Give four special occasions on which the Qur'an may be recited.

b What benefits may people get from (i) reciting the Qur'an and (ii) hearing the Qur'an?

Discussion activity 👥

1 Discuss the advantages and disadvantages of holding Qur'an recitation competitions – you may want to find out more about such competitions before you start.

Study tip

Some examination questions will link themes from different parts of this book. You may need to do the same to complete the activities as fully as possible.

The authority of the Qur'an

Beliefs and teachings

This is a scripture in which there is no doubt, a guidance for those who keep evil away.

Qur'an 2:2

Many Muslims believe that the Arabic Qur'an is an earthly copy of the heavenly original. For them it is the word of God and has His **authority**. When Muslims say 'The Qur'an says', what they mean is that 'God says'. The Qur'an can never be wrong according to those who believe that it is the word of God. They believe that it should be used as the basis of the holy law because its commands are God's commands. Many Muslims who hear the words of the Qur'an do not understand what they mean. Scholars, who have studied the Qur'an in great depth, have to translate and explain the words, and work out the laws based on them. These experts do not always agree about what the Qur'an means which is one reason why different Muslims follow Islam in different ways.

The power of the Qur'an

Muslims believe that the Qur'an brings the power of God into this world and that those who are spiritually aware can feel God's presence in its words. For them the Qur'an is proof of God's existence because only these words have that hidden depth. The power that comes through the words is so strong that people come to believe in the Muslim faith just by reading or hearing those words.

B *'In the name of God, The Merciful and The Compassionate.' Muslims start any recitation of the Qur'an with these words to show that they are speaking on God's behalf*

∞ links

See page 30 on the Shari'ah for information about how the law is worked out from the Qur'an.

To learn more about the role of the Imam, see Chapter 3, pages 66–67.

Research activity 🔍

2 According to tradition, Caliph Umar was converted to Islam just by hearing the Qur'an. The 1960s pop star Cat Stevens (now Yusuf Islam) was also converted in this way. Find out more about their stories, or the stories of others converted by the Qur'an.

C *Yusuf Islam, formerly the pop star Cat Stevens*

Summary

You should now understand the importance of the recitation of the Qur'an, and be aware that the Qur'an has absolute authority as a record of the words of God. Scholars interpret those words to discover their meaning for today.

D *The Qur'an has God's authority*

Hadith

The **hadith** and the **sunnah** are the two main sources of authority in Islam after the Qur'an. A hadith is a saying of the Prophet. These sayings were passed down by word of mouth for over 200 years before being collected and recorded in writing. Great care was taken to examine each saying to make sure that it was genuine before it was officially recorded. One of the most important collections was made by a man named Bukhari.

The Prophet's sayings cover a wide range of topics including beliefs and rituals, and rules about daily life. Some of the sayings show what Muhammad commanded the Muslims to do or allowed them to do, and what he discouraged them from doing or forbade them to do. The sayings are used alongside the Qur'an as a basis of the Shari'ah.

Beliefs and teachings

The Prophet said, 'Whoever is not merciful to others will not be treated mercifully.'

Hadith

The Prophet said, 'Whoever fasts during Ramadan with faith and seeking his reward from Allah will have his past sins forgiven.'

Hadith

Hadith Qudsi

Some of the sayings are known as Hadith Qudsi. These contain words that Muhammad said he had received from God which are not part of the Qur'an.

Beliefs and teachings

On the authority of Abu Harayrah who said that the Prophet said that Allah said:

Spend on charity, O son of Adam, and I shall spend on you.

It was collected by Bukhari.

This is a typical Hadith Qudsi. The record tells us who heard Muhammad say these words, gives us the words themselves and says who collected the saying.

Sunnah

Muhammad taught by example as much as by words. Muhammad's actions are his sunnah and his sunnah is the example that Muslims should follow. The sunnah is passed on from generation to generation as parents teach their children what they must do as Muslims, and is recorded in the stories of Muhammad's life and in his sayings.

Objectives

Know what is meant by hadith and sunnah.

Study examples of hadith and sunnah.

Consider the importance of hadith and sunnah.

Key terms

Hadith: sayings of the Prophet Muhammad. A major source of Islamic law.

Sunnah: the teachings and deeds of Muhammad.

Discussion activity

1. a How reliable do you think is any story that has been passed on by word of mouth?

   b Would it make a difference if it had been learned by heart by each person?

A *Giving is part of Muhammad's sunnah*

Beliefs and teachings

You have in the Messenger of Allah a beautiful pattern of conduct for any one whose hope is in Allah and in the Final day.

Qur'an 33:21

The sunnah includes the detailed movements and exact times of the daily prayers, and customs and manners like standing when a funeral procession passes, or thanking God before starting a meal. Many Muslims try to model themselves as closely as possible on Muhammad's example. He is their role model.

Activities

1. Explain what is meant by a hadith.
2. Give **one** example of a hadith.
3. Give **one** reason why hadiths are important.
4. Explain what is meant by sunnah.
5. Give **one** example of Muhammad's sunnah.
6. Give **one** reason why Muhammad's sunnah is important.

B The detailed positions for prayer are based on the Prophet's sunnah

Study tip

Make sure your example of a hadith is very different from your example of sunnah. It is very easy to get confused.

Muhammad's sunnah

During a journey, the Prophet ordered his companions to prepare a sheep for eating. One said, 'I will kill it'; another said, 'I will skin it'; another said, 'I will cook it.' The Prophet said, 'I will gather the firewood.' Hearing this, the men said, 'Messenger of God, you don't need to work; we will do whatever is to be done.' Muhammad replied, 'I know that you would do for me whatever is to be done, but I do not like to be set apart from you. God does not like to see his servant setting himself above his companions.'

Case study

The authority of the hadith and the sunnah

Some Muslims believe that the hadith has as much authority as the Qur'an. This is because they believe that all prophets were perfect from the moment they were called by God, and that the sayings were correctly recorded. Other Muslims do not accept this. Some believe that Muhammad was perfect as a prophet but, like all human beings, could make mistakes in the rest of his life. Others believe that the record of these sayings is not trustworthy because human beings can forget or change sayings as they pass them on.

Muhammad's sunnah is accepted as a perfect guide by many Muslims based on their understanding of Qur'an 33:21. However, others believe that all the guidance they need is in the Qur'an. To support their argument, they point to the way the Qur'an describes itself as 'The Book explained in detail' (Qur'an 6:114) and 'The Book explaining all things' (Qur'an 116:89). Some Muslims also point out that Muhammad lived over 1400 years ago and that his example is in some ways very out of date.

C Some men believe that following Muhammad's sunnah means you must allow your beard to grow long

Discussion activities

2. Read the case study which describes an event in the life of Muhammad. What lessons do you think Muslims could learn from this story?
3. How can an example set so long ago still be relevant today?

Summary

You should now know that a hadith is a saying of Muhammad, and the sunnah is the custom of Muhammad. Together with the Qur'an, they form the basis for Shari'ah law.

Introduction to the life of Muhammad

A *Saudi Arabia*

Objectives

Know and understand the social and religious background to Muhammad's career and the main events of his early life.

Key terms

Muhammad: the last and greatest of the prophets of Allah. The name Muhammad means 'praised'.

Birth and early life

Muhammad, the man whom Muslims believe to be the final prophet of God, was born in Makkah in what is now Saudi Arabia, around 570 CE. His father died before he was born, and his mother before he was six, so he was brought up by his uncle Abu Talib. Abu Talib was an important man in Makkah because he was the head of one of the clans. A clan was a group of families who were all related to each other. A group of clans made up a tribe. Muhammad was born into the Hashim clan which was part of the Quraysh tribe. This was the ruling tribe of Makkah.

Research activity

Find out about the climate of Saudi Arabia so that you can imagine the difficulties people would have faced living there over 1400 years ago.

B *Traders like Muhammad would have loaded their goods on to camels to cross the desert*

C *Desert conditions are very harsh. Life is only possible where there is a source of water*

Muhammad entered the family business and became a trader. He built up a reputation for being trustworthy and honest, and made good profits on his trading trips abroad. In 595 CE, when he was 25, he married Khadijah, a wealthy widow, and started a family. It seemed as though he had everything he could wish for.

■ Social situation

Muhammad was troubled by the way of life and the social conditions of the people of Makkah. Some people thought that they were superior to others just because of the clan and tribe they belonged to; some of the traders were dishonest and cheated their customers; the richer people were not sharing their wealth with the poor; people gambled; and drunkenness and violence were common. Women were particularly badly treated and unwanted female babies were sometimes simply left in the desert to die.

■ Religious situation

The people's religious life also concerned him. They knew about God but, to them, He was only one of many gods that could be worshipped. Each of these gods was represented by a small statue or object called an idol. 360 idols were kept in the central shrine, called the Ka'aba. The people did not seem to care about religion. Also, they did not believe there was life after death, when they would be rewarded or punished for their life on earth. Muhammad believed that there was only one God, but he did not completely agree with the beliefs of the Christians or Jews he met on his trading journeys.

∞**links**

To find out more about the importance of Makkah for Muslims today, see Chapter 2, pages 48–49.

D *Idols such as these were kept in the Ka'aba*

∞**links**

See the Glossary for a definition of the term 'Ka'aba'.

Activities

1 Start your own dateline for the life of Muhammad. Two dates are mentioned on these pages, find them and note briefly what happened in Muhammad's life at that date. You can add to this later.

2 Muslims call the time before Muhammad began his work 'the days of ignorance' (Jahiliyyah). Why do you think they gave it this name?

Summary

You should now know and understand the social and religious background to Muhammad's career and the main events of his early life.

Study tip

Remember that time is limited for any one question in an examination. Focus on the key facts about the background to Muhammad's career, rather than smaller details about his life.

1.9 Muhammad in Makkah

Muhammad's call to be a prophet

A The Hira cave outside Makkah. You can see how dry and rocky the area around Makkah is from this picture

Objectives

Know and understand the importance of Muhammad's career in Makkah.

Consider different interpretations of his call to be a prophet.

Muhammad used to take time out for spiritual reflection by spending time alone in a cave on Mount Hira, just outside Makkah. He was there during the month of Ramadan in 610 CE when he became aware of a presence and a voice which urged him to read or recite some words. Muhammad, like many others at the time, could not read, so he shouted 'I cannot'. He felt himself being squeezed until he was nearly dead, then released. The demand came again 'read' and again he shouted 'I cannot'. He felt himself being squeezed again but this time, when he was released, the voice commanded him to recite the words now found in the Qur'an.

Beliefs and teachings

In the name of God who creates, creates man from a clot of blood.

And God is the Most Generous who teaches by the pen, teaches man what he knew not.

Qur'an 96:1–5

Muhammad repeated the words and then left the cave in terror. He had seen no one but he felt as though the words he had heard were burned into him. Then an Angel appeared and the same voice he had heard in the cave told him, 'You are the Messenger of God, and I am Jibril.' Muhammad fled home to his wife, frightened and confused. He needed Khadijah to reassure him that he was not mad. She comforted him and the next day she took him to meet her Christian cousin. When he heard Muhammad's story, he knew that what had appeared to him had also appeared to the earlier prophets and that Muhammad had been chosen by God.

links

To read verses in the Qur'an that describe Muhammad as a Messenger of Allah and the Seal of the Prophets, see pages 28–29.

Study tip

Make sure you can give a clear outline account of Muhammad's call to be a prophet. It is a very important event.

Research activity

Using the internet, find out more about Muslim beliefs in angels, and particularly about Jibril.

Extension activity

1 a Why do you think many people did not believe that Muhammad had really received a message from God?

b What evidence could support the idea that it was a message from God?

■ Early preaching

Muhammad now knew that he had a mission from God, but it was not clear to him what the mission was. He was told to warn the people that God would judge them and he began by sharing the message with his family and friends. In 613 CE, God commanded him to preach openly and to invite everyone to believe in the One God, Allah. As soon as he did, the leaders in Makkah started attacking Muhammad and his followers.

Beliefs and teachings

Many of the early verses of the Qur'an criticise the social and religious errors of the time

Those who do right will be in delight, those who do wrong will burn in the fires of hell.

Qur'an 82:13–15

Woe to the cheats, who demand full measure when they take from men, but give only part measure when they weigh goods out for them.

Qur'an 83:1–3

Remember the name of God and devote yourself with complete devotion. Lord of the West and the East, there is no God but Him, so choose God alone as your defender.

Qur'an 74:8–9

B   *The Ka'aba in Makkah*

■ Opposition

Historians think there are many reasons why the leaders in Makkah opposed Muhammad.

- Makkah was a successful trading centre because it was a shrine. Once every year, people from the surrounding areas and countries would come to the Ka'aba to make a pilgrimage to the idols and to trade with each other. The local leaders thought that if Muhammad stopped idol worship they would lose all of this, because then no one would come to the Ka'aba.

- All Arabs were proud of the customs and traditions of their ancestors, and Muhammad was attacking these. He was also attacking their beliefs.

- Muhammad was challenging their power because people were following him instead of them.

The leaders called Muhammad mad and accused him of inventing the Qur'an. They mocked and harassed him whenever they could, and abused and tortured the Muslims who did not come from powerful clans. They could not attack Muhammad himself because his clan stood by him. When these tactics did not stop him, they tried to bribe him with promises of power. Then they offered to leave him alone if he would publicly approve of their idol worship. The rulers of Makkah even tried banning everyone from having any contact with Muhammad and his followers. However, when the Muslims started to suffer because of this, the ordinary people broke the ban. Nothing would stop Muhammad from preaching what he believed to be the truth.

Activities

1   Add the new dates to your dateline and note the events that happened at each time.

2   Explain why the leaders in Makkah thought Muhammad was mad.

3   Suggest how the example Muhammad set in Makkah can help Muslims living in non-Muslim countries today.

Summary

You should now know about and understand the importance of Muhammad's career in Makkah. You should also know there have been different interpretations of his call to be a prophet.

The year of sorrow: 619 CE

Muhammad had been relatively safe so far, because he had the support of the head of his clan and the comfort and support of his wife. In 619 CE he lost both when his uncle and wife died. One of Muhammad's greatest enemies, his uncle Abu Lahab, was the new head of the clan, and he expelled Muhammad. Now Muhammad could be killed without his murderers fearing any consequences. It seemed as if Muhammad's mission could fail.

The Hijrah: 622 CE

In 620 CE a small group of people from Yathrib, a city about 250 miles to the north, heard Muhammad preach. They spread the message and in 622 CE representatives of the city invited Muhammad to be their leader. Muslims began to leave Makkah to start a new life. Finally Muhammad himself escaped. This event is known as the **Hijrah**. The day Muhammad left Makkah was made the first day of the Islamic calendar because it was the birth of a new community, one ruled by God and the Prophet. Each year is counted AH, meaning after Hijrah.

A *The journey from Makkah to Madinah*

The Hijrah showed what God expected from Muslims:

- obedience and loyalty to God;
- loyalty to the Prophet to come first above loyalty to the family;
- Islam to be a complete way of life and not something that could l limited to beliefs and special practices at special times.

Muhammad in Madinah

Muhammad was both Prophet and head of state in Yathrib, which became known as **Madinah**, meaning The City. As Prophet, he led the prayers and continued to pass on the revelations as they arrived. One revelation changed the direction of prayer from Jerusalem to Makkah which showed that the city had a large part to play in the future of Islam. As head of state, he ruled the community on God's behalf. For many Muslims, Madinah is the model of what an Islamic society should be.

Key terms

Hijrah: the emigration of the Prophet Muhammad from Makkah to Madinah in 622 CE; the Muslim calendar commences from this event.

Madinah (Medina): Muhammad travelled to Madinah from Makkah in 622 CE. It is regarded as the second holiest city in Islam and is the burial place of Muhammad.

Research activity

1 Find out what today's date is according to the Muslim calendar.

August Sha'ban/Ramadam 1431						
S	M	T	W	T	F	S
1	2	3	4	5	6	7
20	21	22	23	24	25	26
8	9	10	11	12	13	14
27	28	29	RM	2	3	4
15	16	17	18	19	20	21
5	6	7	8	9	10	11
22	23	24	25	26	27	28
12	13	14	15	16	17	18
29	30	31				
19	20	21				

B *August 2010 in the Muslim calendar is Sha'ban/Ramadan 1431 AH*

Study tip

You will need to know about the Hijrah and its importance for Muslims.

Uniting the community

He had to unite the community which was not an easy task. The people included the Muslim migrants from Makkah, the Muslims of Madinah known as the Ansar, and others who had not yet accepted Islam. Muhammad set up a framework of duties and rights which each group agreed to. He established the brotherhood of believers between the Ansar and the migrants, and the Ansar agreed to share their shelter, food and money with the new arrivals. The rules of the community were revealed, covering such things as marriage, divorce and women's rights.

Defending the community

As head of state, Muhammad was also a military leader and there were many battles with the army of Makkah: the battle of Badr in 624 CE, the battle of Uhud in 625 CE, and the battle of the Trench in 627 CE. The people of Makkah tried to destroy Madinah in 627 CE but Muhammad avoided bloodshed by ordering his men to dig a large trench around the city. When the army arrived from Makkah, it found that it had been outsmarted and left. The city was safe but any Muslim found outside its walls was likely to be captured and killed.

C   *The Mosque of The Prophet, Madinah. This magnificent mosque stands on the site of a mosque originally built by Mohammad next to his house in Madinah*

Beliefs and teachings

The relationship between believers

The believers are protecting friends of one another; they command the right and forbid the wrong, and they establish worship and pay the poor due, and they obey God and his messenger.

Qur'an 9:71

Research activities

2   Find out more about the battles of Badr, Uhud and the Trench. Research the teaching of the Qur'an on the use of force.

3   Suggest why Muhammad approved the use of force on these occasions, but why he tried to avoid as much bloodshed as possible.

Summary

You should now know the events of the Hijrah and understand the significance of the Hijrah for Muslims. You should also be able to outline the role of Muhammad in Madinah as Prophet and head of state.

Activities

1   Add the dates from this page to your dateline and make a note of what happened at each time.

2   Copy out the following sentences, fitting each of these words, dates or phrases into the correct gap:

622 CE   divorce   head of state   Hijrah   laws

Madinah   marriage   military leader

Muhammad emigrated from Makkah to _____ in the year _____. This event is known as the _____.
Muhammad was more than a Prophet in this city, he was also the _____ and a _____. Verses of the Qur'an were revealed which contained the _____ for the new community. Some of these were about _____ and _____.

The Muslims needed freedom of movement outside Madinah in order to spread Islam. To do that, they had to deal with the problem of Makkah. In 628 CE Muhammad led a large group of Muslims to Makkah as pilgrims. The people of Makkah refused them entry but then they agreed a treaty with Muhammad. Six years before, he and his supporters had left Makkah with almost nothing. Now the people of Makkah were treating him as an equal.

The key terms of the treaty were:

- a 10-year peace deal in which each side agreed not to attack the other;
- permission for Muslims to enter Makkah for pilgrimage from the following year onwards;
- permission for the people of Makkah to visit Madinah.

The treaty meant that more people could hear the message of Islam and the number of Muslims began to grow. In 630 CE, when the people of Makkah broke the treaty, Muhammad led a huge army against them. When he arrived at the city, the leaders simply surrendered and agreed to accept the rule of Islam. One of Muhammad's first acts as ruler was to order that all the idols in the Ka'aba should be smashed and the shrine rededicated to God.

Objectives

Know how Islam was spread outside Madinah.

Explain the importance of Muhammad as the final prophet of Islam.

The last years

In the last two years of his life, Muhammad continued to spread the word of Islam until the whole area had accepted him as leader. He also carried out one full pilgrimage to Makkah, during which the last verses of the Qur'an were revealed.

> **Beliefs and teachings**
>
> This day I have perfected your religion for you and completed my favour on you, and have chosen Islam for you as your religion.
>
> *Qur'an* 5:3

Muslims believe that with this final verse God completed his revelations to human beings. Muhammad died after a short illness in June 632 CE. He was buried in a simple grave in Madinah.

The last of the prophets

> **Beliefs and teachings**
>
> Muhammad is not the father of any man among you, but he is the messenger of Allah and the Seal of the Prophets.
>
> *Qur'an* 33:40

A   *Muhammad's tomb lies beneath the green dome of the Prophet's Mosque*

When Muslims call Muhammad 'the Seal of the Prophets' they are comparing him to a seal that would be put at the end of a document to show that it was complete. They believe that he is the last of the prophets of God. They believe that, through him, God revealed everything that human beings need to know about what to believe and how they should live. In his last sermon, the Prophet is reported to have said:

Beliefs and teachings

No Prophet or Messenger will come after me and no new religion will be born. I leave behind me two things, the Qur'an and my example. If you follow these you will never go astray.

Hadith

In the shahadah, Muslims do not say that Muhammad *was* the Prophet of God, but that he *is* the Prophet of God. This is because the message he brought is perfectly recorded in the Qur'an, and his sunnah is the guiding example followed by Muslims all over the world.

Beliefs and teachings

You have in the Messenger of Allah a beautiful pattern of conduct for anyone whose hope is in Allah and in the Final day.

Qur'an 33:21

Muslims do not believe that Muhammad was any better than all the other prophets, because all of them obeyed God and delivered his message. Muslims do believe that the revelation given through Muhammad is the only one that was perfectly recorded.

B   *The last verses of the Qur'an were revealed to Muhammad shortly before his death*

∞ links

For more on hadith and sunnah, see pages 20–21.

For an explanation of the shahadah, see Chapter 2, pages 38–39.

Activities

1   Complete the dateline for the life of Muhammad using the dates given here.

2   Answer the following questions:

a   Why was it important for the Muslims to deal with the problem of Makkah?

b   How did the treaty that was agreed in 628 CE help the Muslims?

c   Why did the Muslim army march on Makkah in 630 CE?

d   What does Muhammad's title 'Seal of the Prophets' mean?

e   How was Muhammad similar to and different from the other prophets of Islam?

Summary

You should now know how Islam was spread outside Madinah. You should also be able to explain the importance of Muhammad as the final prophet of Islam.

Study tip

You may need to summarise and explain the Qur'an 33:21 and/or the Qur'an 33:40 in answer to a question in the examination.

Shari'ah

The Shari'ah

The **Shari'ah** is the holy law of Islam based on the laws in the Qur'an and the hadith of the Prophet. About 600 verses of the Qur'an contain laws from God. These cover a range of topics from family life to food, and how to pray and fast. The Qur'an also gives basic principles, like the need to be fair at all times, which guide the scholars in deciding what the law should be. Other laws are found in the hadith.

Case study

Dissection

The Prophet said 'Breaking the bones of the dead is like breaking the bones of the living.' For that reason, Muslim scholars had forbidden the dissection of bodies. However, in recent years, there has been a greater understanding of the good that can come from dissecting bodies, and a new ruling has been given.

Any dissection or operation that has to be done on the dead body for positive reasons is allowable. For example, dissection to gain medical knowledge and dissection in order to find the cause of death to convict criminals. This is to allow the truth (al-Haq) to be discovered, and is based on the Shari'ah principle of establishing justice ('Adil) and to ensure that the guilty do not escape from the punishment as a result of their crimes.

A *Commentaries on the Qur'an interpret its words and apply them to modern situations*

Muslims believe that God alone is the law giver. Only God has the right to say what is right and what is wrong. The work of the scholars was, and still is, to interpret the laws that God has given and to work out what God would want Muslims to do in new situations that arise. This work is very important. Dedicated Muslims want to obey God in everything they do and, to do that, they need to know exactly what God has commanded.

Beliefs and teachings

Laws in the Qur'an

Forbidden to you are animals found dead, blood and the flesh of swine.

Qur'an 5:3

In the light of this verse, Muslims need guidance on various issues today. Should they have blood transfusions? Are they allowed heart transplants? Would God allow them to have a heart valve from a pig if it would save their life? Scholars give judgements about these issues based on their study of all the Qur'an.

When Muslims talk about the Shari'ah today, they often mean the detailed laws that were mostly worked out by scholars in the first 300 years after Muhammad's death. Today there are four schools or traditions of law in Sunni Islam. They vary only in detail; most

B *Should Muslims allow blood transfusions?*

Muslims believe that they are all allowable interpretations of what God has commanded. Shi'ah Muslims only accept the laws developed by the Imams and Shi'ah scholars. Two countries are ruled according to Shari'ah law: Saudi Arabia which is a Sunni country and Iran which is a Shi'ah country. Many others Muslim countries have Shari'ah courts which deal with family matters covered by Shari'ah law like divorce and child custody.

Different views about the Shari'ah

All Muslims want to obey God, but not all Muslims believe that they have to obey the detailed laws worked out by the scholars. They do not think that these laws are God's laws.

Activities

Read the following statements Muslims have made about Shari'ah law. Then write two lists:

1 Statements which support the view that all the Shari'ah laws should be obeyed by all Muslims.

2 Statements which go against the view that all the Shari'ah laws should be obeyed by all Muslims.

a   The Shari'ah has as much authority as the Qur'an.

b   The Shari'ah is the Law of God.

c   The Shari'ah is a law worked out by humans, and humans can be wrong.

d   The rules worked out by the scholars were for their time only. Modern interpretations are needed for today.

e   Only the laws in the Qur'an are God's laws.

f   The Shari'ah laws can never be changed.

> 66 *Shari'ah is permanent for all people all the time. It does not change with time and conditions. For example, drinking wine and gambling are not allowed under Islamic Law. And no-one can change this; it is a law that is valid for all time and for all places.* 99
>
> Islam Beliefs and Teachings, G Sarwar (2008)

> 66 *The Muslim world is in urgent need of new thought … A fresh understanding and a new comprehension of the teachings of the Qur'an and the life and traditions of the Prophet Muhammad.* 99
>
> Introducing Islam, Z Sardar and Z A Malik (2004)

∞ links

To find out more about the differences between Sunni and Shi'ah Islam, see pages 32–33.

The Shari'ah puts all human actions into one of five groups:

Commanded

Approved of

Allowed

Disapproved of

Forbidden

C   Shari'ah laws forbid gambling

Summary

You should now understand that the Shari'ah is the Islamic law based on the Qur'an and the hadith. You should also understand that while some Muslims see it as the law of God, others think it is a human law which does not always have to be obeyed.

Study tip

It will help your understanding of Shari'ah if you are able to find an example of a law found in the Qur'an or sunnah, and an example of one decided by the scholars.

The Sunnis

After Muhammad died, there were different opinions about how Islam should be led and what authority the leader should have. The majority believed that only the Qur'an and the sunnah had the authority to tell people what to believe and what to do. They decided to elect a leader who would act on behalf of God and the Prophet, and make sure that people obeyed God's laws. This leader would be called a Caliph. The first three Caliphs elected by the community were Abu Bakr, Umar and Uthman.

Key terms

Sunni: Muslims who believe in the successorship of Abu Bakr, Umar, Uthman and Ali.

Imam: in Shi'ah, the title of Ali and his successors.

Shi'ah (Shi'i): Muslims who believe in the Imamah, successorship of Ali.

A *Sunni Muslims claim to follow only the Qur'an and the sunnah*

The Caliphs were not law makers, they were law enforcers. The laws were worked out by the scholars who studied the Qur'an, the hadith and the sunnah. The community as a whole considered, and then accepted or rejected, their conclusions about exactly what God had commanded the Muslims to do. This group were later called **Sunni** Muslims meaning followers of the sunnah.

The twelve Imams

1 Ali d.40 A.H.
2 Hasan d.61 A.H.
3 Husayn d.69 A.H.
4 Ali d.95 A.H.
5 Muhammad d.114 A.H.
6 Ja'far d.148 A.H.
7 Musa d.183 A.H.
8 Ali d.203 A.H.
9 Muhammad d.220 A.H.
10 Ali d.254 A.H.
11 Hasan d.260 A.H.
12 Muhammad Al-Mahdi (The Hidden Imam)

The Shi'ah

A second group believed that Muhammad had named Ali to be his successor. Ali was his cousin and one of the earliest converts to Islam. He was also married to Muhammad's daughter, Fatimah. Ali and his supporters believed that the true leader had to be chosen by God. They also believed that God would give Ali the authority to make new laws and give new teaching. This leader, called the **Imam**, had to be a descendent of Muhammad. Each Imam would identify the next one before he died. Ali's claims to be the leader chosen by God were ignored by many Muslims. As time went on, Islam split between the party of Ali, now known as the **Shi'ah**, and the Sunni Muslims. The Shi'ah Muslims have their own interpretation of the Shari'ah laws and

B   *Iranian Shi'ah Muslims pray for the return of the Hidden Imam*

Research activity

Find out more about the main teachings of Shi'ah Islam. If using an internet search engine, it may be useful to try searching for both 'Shi'ah' and the alternative spelling 'Shia'. Some interesting websites may only recognise one of these two forms of spelling.

only accept those hadith which have been passed down through Ali or his followers. They do not accept that the first three Caliphs were the rightful rulers of Islam.

Shi'ah Muslims believe that they are still guided by an Imam today. He is the Hidden Imam. They believe that by a miracle, God has taken the Hidden Imam into hiding somewhere on earth and kept him alive over the centuries. The Hidden Imam is believed to communicate spiritually with the religious leaders.

Sunni Islam rules itself by the Qur'an and sunnah as interpreted by the community of believers. It has no overall leader today.

C   *Iranian religious teachers called Ayatollahs are believed to be the spokesmen for the Hidden Imam*

Activity

The idea of the Caliph is very different from the idea of the Imam. Put the word Caliph as a heading on the right-hand side of a page and Imam as a heading on the left-hand side. Under each heading, list the key points about each one: how they were chosen; what authority they had; what role they had to carry out.

Study tip

At the end of an examination, if you have time, check your answers to make sure that you have said what you meant to say and to see whether there is anything else you could say or an example that you could give.

Summary

You should now be able to explain the differing views of authority and leadership held by Sunni and Shi'ah Muslims.

1

Beliefs and sources of authority – summary

For the examination, you should now be able to:

✔ understand the key beliefs and sources of authority that underpin the Muslim way of life and influence their behaviour and attitudes

✔ know and understand the terms Islam, Muslim, Allah and tawhid

✔ recall and explain Muslim beliefs about risalah and akhirah and consider their importance

✔ recall Muslim accounts of the revelation and compilation of the Qur'an

✔ know and understand the recitation of the Qur'an and its authority

✔ explain what is meant by hadith and sunnah, and consider their importance

✔ recall the main events in the life of Muhammad and consider their importance, in particular:
  – the background to his work
  – his call to be a prophet
  – the Hijrah
  – his work in Madinah (Medina) and Makkah (Mecca)
  – his importance as the last of the prophets

✔ explain what is meant by Shari'ah and consider the importance of the Shari'ah

✔ explain the differing views of authority held by Sunni and Shi'ah Muslims.

Sample answer

1 Write an answer to the following examination question:

'It is unreasonable to believe in life after death today.'
Do you agree? Give reasons for your answer, showing that you have thought about more than one point of view. *(6 marks)*

2 Read the following sample answer:

> I agree. There is no proof. People imagine that they see ghosts or hear dead people talking to them. No one wants to die so they hope they won't.
>
> On the other hand, the Qur'an is God's words. God says there is life after death so there has to be.

3 With a partner, discuss the sample answer. To achieve the top level you need to give a 'well argued response'. How do you think this answer could be improved so that it is better argued?

4 What mark would you give this answer out of 6? Look at the mark scheme in the Introduction on page 7 (AO2). What are the reasons for the mark you have given?

Practice questions

1   Look at the photograph below and answer the following questions.

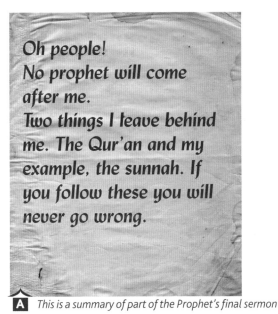

A   *This is a summary of part of the Prophet's final sermon*

(a)   What does the word Qur'an mean?   *(2 marks)*

(b)   'The Qur'an is the only guide to life a Muslim needs.'
     What do you think? Explain your opinion.   *(3 marks)*

Study tip   To gain 3 marks, you must give one developed reason for your answer or several simple reasons.

(c)   Explain what Islam teaches about prophets of God.   *(6 marks)*

(d)   Explain why Muhammad is thought to be more important than the earlier prophets of Islam.   *(4 marks)*

(e)   'Muhammad lived over 1400 years ago; his example is not relevant to today.'
     Do you agree? Give reasons for your answer, showing that you have thought about more than one point of view.   *(6 marks)*

Study tip   Make sure that you have considered at least two different points of view.

2 The Five Pillars of Islam

2.1 Introduction to The Five Pillars

Islam is based on five things, declaring that there is no god but Allah and that Muhammad is the messenger of Allah; performing prayers; the payment of Zakah; the pilgrimage and fasting in the month of Ramadan.

Hadith Bukhari

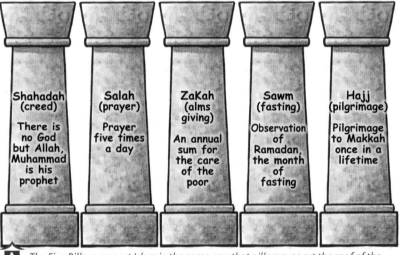

A The Five Pillars support Islam in the same way that pillars support the roof of the prayer hall

B The Five Pillars

Arabic name	Meaning	How often must this be done?
Shahadah	Declaration of faith	Throughout your life
Salah	Ritual prayer	Five times each day
Zakah	Welfare payment	Once a year
Sawm	Fasting in Ramadan	One month a year
Hajj	Pilgrimage to Makkah	Once a lifetime

The duties in Table **B** are known as **The Five Pillars of Islam** because they support Islam just as physical pillars support the roof of the prayer hall in the mosque. Muslims believe that God has commanded them to do these duties for their own good. They believe that by doing them they will become better Muslims and Islam will become stronger. Islam is the way of obedience to God and it is a complete way of life. The word Muslim means a person who has submitted the whole of their life to God. Whatever they are doing, Muslims must do it in the way God has commanded. The Five Pillars help them to do this and can be seen as spiritual training exercises.

The way in which each pillar supports Islam is covered later in this chapter. Dr Chris Hewer, a non-Muslim writer, thinks the development of 'God-consciousness' is the purpose of the pillars:

> 66 *These practices are a training programme to build God-consciousness within the Muslim so that she or he may be led into the perfect state of Islam and thus both be happy in this life and rewarded with paradise in the hereafter.* 99
>
> *Understanding Islam, C T R Hewer (2006)*

When Muslims have God-consciousness they are always aware that God is with them and watching all they do. This is said to be the key to success in Islam and the pillars are seen as the key to developing it. This means that the pillars of Islam are the key to living a perfect Muslim life. In this chapter, as each pillar is explored in turn, there are a few general questions you can keep in mind. Are all of the five pillars equally important? Does it matter if you simply cannot do one or more of them? In what other ways could they help you to become a better Muslim?

Activity

2 Write out each of the following statements, filling in the blank as you do so.

a The pillar that only needs to be done once in a lifetime is _____ .

b The pillar that has to be done five times a day is _____ .

c The pillar that is done one month a year is _____ .

d The pillar that has to be done throughout life is _____ .

e The pillar that is done once a year is _____ .

Discussion activity

In what ways could being aware that God is watching you at all times make someone a better Muslim?

C *Salah ritual – prayer*

D *Zakah – welfare payment*

G *Shahadah – declaration of faith*

E *Sawm – fasting in Ramadan*

F *Hajj – pilgrimage to Makkah*

Summary

You should now know that the Five Pillars of Islam are named shahadah, salah, zakah, sawm and hajj. You should also be able to explain their meaning. They are designed to support Islam and to make people better Muslims.

2.2 Shahadah

The first pillar is the duty to declare the two great beliefs of Islam. These beliefs are: the Oneness of God, and prophethood. Muslims carry out this duty by making sure that the Arabic words of the **shahadah** can be seen and heard repeatedly in the world of Islam. They appear on flags, on mosque walls, in public buildings and in homes. They are the first words said to a baby after birth; they are repeated in the call to prayer and in the prayers themselves. They should be the final words Muslims speak or hear before they die. In English these words are: There is no god but Allah, and Muhammad is the Prophet of Allah.

Objectives

Recall and explain what the shahadah is and how Muslims should carry out this duty.

Key terms

Shahadah: Muslim declaration of faith. The first pillar of Islam.

A The Saudi Arabian flag shows the shahadah

B Muslim father whispering the declaration of faith in his baby's ear

The shahadah is the foundation of Islam. Anyone who stands in front of witnesses and makes this statement of faith is considered a Muslim. This is not because the words have any type of supernatural power to make you a Muslim. It is because when you say them you are dedicating your life to the one God and accepting that Muhammad is the way God has made himself and his laws known. Saying the words of the shahadah is pointless if you do not mean what they say and do not intend to live as if they are true.

The shahadah has a special place among the pillars; it is the foundation of Islam. The other four pillars simply put the two statements of faith into practice. They help Muslims to develop the strengths they will need if they are going to live up to their faith. Mawdudi, a Muslim scholar, sums up the importance of the shahadah when he says:

⊂⊃ links

For more information on Muslim beliefs about the Oneness of God and prophethood, see Chapter 1, pages 8–13.

Beliefs and teachings

The Shahadah

There is no god but Allah, and Muhammad is the Prophet of Allah.

> 66 Believe it and you enter Islam on its strength; understand it fully and mould your lives on it and you become true Muslims. Without it you can neither enter nor remain in Islam. 99
>
> Let us be Muslims, S A A Mawdudi (1982)

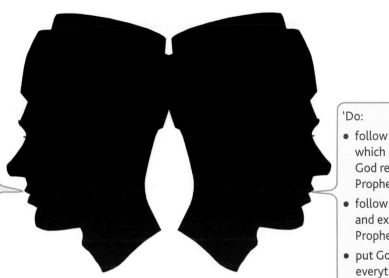

'Do not:

- worship any idols or other gods
- follow the example of other people when it conflicts with Islam
- treat anything in your life as more important than God.'

'Do:

- follow the Qur'an which is the Word of God revealed to the Prophet Muhammad
- follow the teaching and example of the Prophet
- put God first in everything you do.'

   C   *How to show the shahadah in practice*

Those Muslims who repeat and live out the words of the shahadah are witnesses to their faith. Outsiders learn what Islam teaches and how God expects people to live, by hearing and watching what Muslims say and do.

The shahadah in Shi'ah Islam

Some Shi'ah Muslims add a third phrase to the shahadah. They declare 'There is no god but Allah, Muhammad is the Prophet of Allah, and Ali is the Friend of God.' This shows their belief that Ali, Muhammad's cousin and son-in-law, was the only true successor of Muhammad and that only he and his descendents know the true meaning of the revelation given to Muhammad. They believe that only they have a true understanding of how God wants people to live.

Extension activity

Use the internet to find out about 'shirk', which is the sin of denying the Oneness of God.

∞ links

For more information about Shi'ah Islam, see Chapter 1, pages 32–33.

Activities

1   What are the **two** statements of faith that make up the shahadah?
2   Write down **two** occasions on which the shahadah would be spoken.
3   Write down **two** places where the shahadah is often displayed.
4   Muslims must show that they are following the shahadah by how they live. Give **two** examples of how they do this.

Summary

You should now know that the shahadah is the Islam declaration of faith, and that this duty should be constantly repeated and acted on. Muslims who repeat and act on the shahadah will be witnesses to their faith.

Study tip

You will need to remember lots of facts for the examination. Practise remembering whenever you can – write out the key Arabic words and their meanings on small cards then use the cards to test yourself.

Muslims have a duty to pray to God at five set times each day. This is the duty of salah, the second pillar of Islam. **Salah** means 'connection' or 'contact' and, when they pray, Muslims take time out to focus on God and on what he expects of them.

Prayer times

Muslim scholars work out the times of the five daily prayers based on the times of sunrise and sunset. This means that the times change each day and from place to place, even in the same country. In Britain, winter prayer times are very different from summer prayer times; prayer times in London are different from prayer times in Manchester. Shi'ah Muslims combine the midday and afternoon prayers, and the sunset and night prayers, so they have only three prayer times a day. Each prayer is announced by the call to prayer, which used to come only from a mosque but which can now be heard from mobile phones, alarm clocks and the radio.

A *Prayer times*

Fajr	Just before sunrise
Zuhr	Just after midday
Asr	Afternoon
Maghrib	Sunset
Isha	Night

Wudu

Beliefs and teachings

When you go to pray, wash your faces, and your hands up to the elbows. You must lightly rub your heads and wash your feet up to the ankles.

Qur'an 5:6

Muslims are commanded to prepare for prayer by performing a purification ritual called **wudu**. There are detailed instructions about how this should be done and mosques provide either a fountain or special rooms for this purpose.

Objectives

Explain the meaning of salah and how Muslims prepare for prayer.

Key terms

Salah: prayer with and worship of Allah, performed under the conditions set by the Prophet Muhammad. The second pillar of Islam.

Wudu: ritual washing before prayer.

Study tip

Make sure you can outline how Muslims perform wudu. You could draw diagrams to illustrate each stage.

B *Prayer times*

links

See Chapter 3 for more information about the facilities mosques provide.

C   *Young Muslim boys performing wudu*

When it is not possible to use water, a dry form of purification is allowed. This shows that the most important purpose of wudu is not to make a person physically clean (although being clean is very important when so many people meet so closely together). The main purpose of wudu is to help the Muslim prepare spiritually.

The spiritual purpose of wudu

- To separate prayer from the other activities of life and help Muslims focus on God.
- To remind them of how great God is.
- To help them admit to any way in which they have failed God since their last prayer.

Facing Makkah

Muslims turn to face Makkah when they pray. This means that they are both physically and mentally focused on this single point on earth in the same way that their life should be focused only on God. All Muslims, wherever they are, turn to face that point when they are ready to pray. They can pray anywhere as long as it is clean. However, many prefer to pray in a mosque or at least with other Muslims.

∞ links

To understand more about the mihrab, see Chapter 3, pages 60–61.

Extension activity

Use the internet to find out how Muslims perform wudu. Write a leaflet for non-Muslims, which explains wudu and its importance.

Discussion activity

Do you think doing wudu helps Muslims to pray, or does it make the daily prayers more difficult?

D   *A mihrab in a mosque showing the direction of Makkah*

Activities

1   According to the Qur'an, which parts of the body should be washed before prayer?

2   When is the earliest prayer of the day?

3   Why could it be difficult for some Muslims to perform the earliest prayer?

Summary

You should now know that the second pillar of Islam is the duty to pray five times each day. Salah means contact prayers. Muslims prepare for prayer by performing wudu and facing Makkah.

Rak'ahs

There is a set sequence of actions and words for prayer called a **rak'ah**, and the sequence is repeated a set number of times at each of the five daily prayers. The main parts of a rak'ah are:

- stand and recite the first chapter of the Qur'an;
- bow to show how great God is;
- prostrate to show complete obedience to God.

A *These Muslims are prostrating themselves to show their complete obedience to God*

When Muslims pray at a mosque or in a group they stand closely together in rows facing Makkah and do these movements at the same time. This is an impressive sight. They are showing that they are united as a community because they all do the same actions at the same time. They are showing how great God is, how they submit to him by bowing and prostrating themselves. They are following the example of the Prophet by copying his actions.

Jumuah prayers

The **Jumuah** prayer is the Friday midday prayer. It is held at the mosque and all male Muslims must attend. Women do not have to attend but may do so if they wish. The Imam will lead the prayers and he also delivers a sermon which reminds the worshippers of their duty to God. Friday is not a day of rest in Islam and the daily routine carries on as normal. However, Muslim shops and businesses will shut over lunchtime to allow employees to go to the prayers.

Du'a prayers

These are personal prayers. They can be offered at any time, anywhere, and are often added on to the end of the prayer ritual. Although formal prayers are in Arabic, Muslims may use their own language and their

Objectives

Explain how Muslims pray and consider the importance of prayer.

Key terms

Rak'ah: a sequence of movements in ritual prayer.

Jumuah: weekly communal salah performed after midday on a Friday.

Du'a: personal prayer.

B *The prostration position has to be learned in detail*

 links

See the Glossary for a definition of the term 'prostration'.

Research activity

Find out how many rak'ahs are performed at each daily prayer and exactly how prostration should be carried out. Do you think having set movements and words is a good idea?

links

To find out more about the Imam, see Chapter 3, pages 66–67.

own words for **du'a** prayers. They use the prayers to praise God, to ask Him for what they need or want, or to thank him for what He has already given to them. In the Qur'an, God says, 'Call on me, I will answer your prayer' (Qur'an 40:60). Muslims pray for such things as success in business, recovery from illness and help in finding what they have lost. They do not always get what they ask for but they believe that God always does what is best for them. One prayer that may be used by someone who is seriously ill is 'Keep me alive as long as it is good for me and give me death when it is good for me.'

The importance of prayer

Muslims believe that these prayers are so important that anyone who stops praying regularly will lose their faith. The contact prayers (salah) make Muslims more aware that God is watching them. This stops them from doing wrong and motivates them to do what God commands. Mawdudi says:

> 66 *You cannot practise Islam unless you believe that God is seeing you all the time and everywhere, that God is aware of all your actions, that God sees you even in darkness, and that God is with you even when you are alone.* 99
>
> *Let us be Muslims, S A A Mawdudi (1982)*

This makes prayer vital if you are to succeed as a Muslim. Prayer unites all Muslims because they are all doing and saying the same regardless of wealth, social status and race. Any Muslim can go into any mosque anywhere in the world and join in the prayers with local Muslims. When they recite the Qur'an in prayer, Muslims are reminded of its teaching. When they prostrate themselves, they are reminded that they are God's servants and that God is greater than them in every way.

D *Many Muslim businesses close at lunchtime for prayers*

Summary

You should now be able to explain how Muslims pray, and you should know the names of the different types of prayer. You should also understand that prayers are an important part of being a successful Muslim.

Study tip

Make sure you can describe how Muslims perform both Jumuah and du'a prayers.

Discussion activity

1 According to Islam, God is all-knowing so he knows what you want before you ask him. What is the point of praying to him?

C *A Muslim woman offering du'a prayers*

Discussion activity

2 Here are four reasons Muslims might give for doing prayers. In groups, decide if each reason is good or bad. Pick out the best and worst reason from the list and explain your answer.

- To impress a future employer
- To please your parents
- To obey God and the Prophet
- To earn forgiveness for your sins

Zakah

The third pillar, **zakah**, is only a duty for richer Muslims. Each year they must pay 2.5 per cent of their savings to the community. In this way they purify their wealth. Zakah means to 'purify' or 'cleanse'. It may seem odd to think of money being 'dirty' and in need of 'cleansing' in some way. Dirty money is money that has been come by dishonestly, perhaps by cheating or by doing something immoral or illegal. Muslims believe that their money is only clean if they have gained it in ways allowed by God's law and have paid God what they owe him.

How much should be paid?

The Qur'an does not say how much should be paid as Zakah, but tells Muslims that whatever they give is good (Qur'an 2:215). Using the Sunna of the Prophet as a guide, scholars have agreed that all Muslims should pay 2.5 per cent of any 'idle wealth' each year. 'Idle wealth' is money you have had for a year but not needed. It may be in the form of cash, savings or jewellery. To work out how much zakah you owe, you need to know the value of the nisab. The nisab is the savings allowance which is based on the value of a small amount of gold. Muslims who have savings lower than the nisab pay no zakah at all. In 2008, the nisab was £1600. You work out your total savings by adding to the sum of cash you hold the value of any gold jewellery you have, the money in your bank or savings account, and any money invested in shares. If the figure is higher than the nisab then you must pay zakah.

Objectives

Explain the pillar of zakah: how it is practised and why it is important.

Key terms

Zakah: purification of wealth by giving to the poor; an act of obligatory worship for Muslims.

Case study

A *According to Islam, if you can afford jewellery like this you should be able to pay zakah*

Calculating how much zakah you should pay

Gold jewellery	£1500
Cash	£50
Bank account	£1000
Shares	none
Total savings	**£2550**

This is higher than the nisab.

2.5% payable = £63.75

How should it be paid?

Zakah may be put in collection boxes at the mosque or paid to a Muslim charity like Muslim Hands. Many Muslims prefer to pay their zakah directly to someone who needs it, but in some Muslim countries Zakah is collected by the government.

How may it be spent?

The Qur'an states how zakah must be spent. It lists people who may receive it, like the poor and needy. It also lists the people whose job it is to collect the money and says that it can be spent 'in God's cause' (Qur'an 9:60). This means that it can be spent in any way that will support Islam and is allowed by God's law.

B   *It is a Muslim duty to help the poor and needy*

Discussion activities

1   Suggest ways in which zakah could be used to spread the message of Islam among non-Muslims.

2   'Giving to the poor encourages them to be lazy.' What do you think? Explain your answer.

Research activity

Find out how Muslim Hands, or another Muslim charity, spends the money people give.

The importance of zakah

- Zakah is a duty to God, commanded in the Qur'an. It reduces the suffering of the poor and needy.
- Zakah trains Muslims to have a healthy attitude to money. They should be generous with what God has given them and not greedy.
- Zakah strengthens the community. It makes sure everyone knows and cares about the problems people face. Also, it increases business in the community by giving more people money to spend.
- The Qur'an makes it clear that those who do not pay the zakah they owe are not true Muslims (Qur'an 5:55).
- The two duties of salah and zakah are linked in the Qur'an. Your prayers should make you feel your love and concern for other Muslims; by paying zakah, you put that feeling into action.

All Muslims are expected to be generous and to give what they can to good causes. Paying zakah is the minimum expected from those who can afford to give. Poorer Muslims are expected to be generous with their time and effort.

Study tip

Good answers about zakah often include clear examples of what the money is used for.

C   *Paying zakah*

Extension activity

'Money is power, and like all power it can be used for good or evil.' This is the theme for a short sermon to be given by an Imam. Prepare notes for the Imam to use. You should include references from the Qur'an, and examples of both good and evil uses for money, in your notes.

Summary

You should now be able to explain what the pillar of zakah is: how it is practised and why it is important. God commands richer Muslims to pay zakah, as this purifies their wealth and supports the whole Muslim community.

Sawm: fasting in the month of Ramadan

The fourth pillar of Islam, **sawm**, is fasting in the month of **Ramadan**. This is both a physical and a spiritual exercise (see the boxes in the margin). In Muslim countries, daily life will carry on as normal but cafés and work canteens will close during the day because no one will eat or drink. The time people usually take up for lunch is spent in prayer, reading the Qur'an or simply socialising with other Muslims. At dusk everything changes, cafés open and happy Muslims get together to break the fast and share time with family and friends. The challenges faced by Muslims in non-Muslim countries like Britain may be harder. Imagine not being able to eat when everyone around you is drinking and snacking.

Key terms

Sawm: fasting from dawn to dusk during Ramadan; sex and smoking are banned when the believer is engaged in this. The fourth pillar of Islam.

Ramadan: month during which fasting from dawn to sunset is demanded (ninth month of the Islamic calendar).

 The evenings of Ramadan are great social occasions, with special food

Fasting is not a duty for everyone. Some people, including pregnant women, nursing mothers, the very young, travellers and those who are ill, are allowed to miss days of fast. However, they must make them up later. Ramadan is sometimes called the annual training programme for Islam. It is also known as the month of the Qur'an because it was during this month that the Qur'an was first revealed. Some Muslims set themselves personal targets, e.g. memorise four chapters of the Qur'an, attend the extra night prayer, stop swearing, phone friends and relatives to see how they are. Devout Muslims may spend the last ten nights of the month at the mosque for prayer and study of the Qur'an.

Fasting as a physical activity

From dawn to dusk, for 30 days of Ramadan:

- No food
- No drink
- No sex
- No smoking

Fasting as a spiritual activity

- Focus on God
- Study the Qur'an
- Improve your submission to God
- Show respect to each other
- Give to charity

Research activities

1. Find out when Ramadan is this year and how long Muslims will be expected to fast each day.

2. Use websites like **www.soundvision.com/info/ramadan** to find out more about how Ramadan is celebrated.

Benefits of Sawm

Beliefs and teachings

You are commanded to fast so that you become God conscious.

Qur'an 2:183

- Muslims are more focused on God because they are making a real effort to obey him all the time during the month of fast. They may take their religion for granted for the rest of the year, but in this month it makes a real difference to them.

- It reminds them of the Qur'an and its teaching. One thirtieth of the Qur'an is recited each night in extra night prayers so that the whole book is recited by the end of the month.

- The community becomes stronger as they all share the challenges and rewards of fasting and come together to break the fast at the end of each day.

- It makes people have sympathy with the poor. Anyone who gets hungry while they are fasting is reminded that some people are hungry all the time. This should make them want to give all they can to help.

- It teaches them self-control and reminds them that serving God must take priority over their own desires.

B   *Traditionally, Muslims eat dates at dusk to break the fast*

C   *Qur'an study can begin at a very early age*

Activity

Each of the following words fills in one of the gaps in the paragraph. Write out the paragraph and put the right word in the right gap: dawn; drink; everything; generous; prayers; Qur'an; Ramadan; swear.

The month of fast which is called _____ is a big challenge for some Muslims who have to work very hard at their self-control. They know that God sees _____ so they cannot cheat. They must not eat or _____ between _____ and dusk. There are also extra _____ in the mosque each night when one thirtieth of the _____ is recited. They also have to make a greater effort than usual to follow all the laws of Islam. No one should _____ at others and everyone should be _____ towards the poor.

Discussion activity

Do you think it would be harder for Muslims to fast in Britain than in a Muslim country?

Extension activity

Research and then write a 'diary' for a day in the life of a Muslim teenager in Britain during Ramadan. Include details to show how challenging fasting can be in a non-Muslim country.

Study tip

Some questions are worth only 2 marks but others are worth up to 6 marks. Check carefully before you start an answer because a short answer may not be enough to earn you full marks.

Summary

You should now understand that fasting in the month of Ramadan is both a physical and a spiritual activity that trains Muslims in their faith. It teaches self-control and generosity, and it reminds them of the teaching of the Qur'an.

2.7   Introduction to the hajj

The **hajj** is the **pilgrimage** to **Makkah** and is the fifth pillar of Islam. A pilgrimage is a sacred or spiritual journey. This journey is a once in a lifetime duty for those Muslims who are healthy and wealthy enough to take part. For many Muslims it is simply too expensive. During one week each year up to three million Muslims come to the Ka'aba as part of the ritual of the hajj.

◼ The Ka'aba

The Great Mosque of Islam is in Makkah in Saudi Arabia. At the centre of the mosque is the Ka'aba, a simple cube-shaped building, the single point that all Muslims from all over the world focus on when they pray. The Qur'an describes the Ka'aba as the first house of worship. It is also known as the House of God or the Sacred House.

A   *The Ka'aba in Makkah*

The design of the Ka'aba is believed to be based on a heavenly model. It is made of bricks and covered in a black cloth on which verses from the Qur'an have been embroidered in gold. The Ka'aba is about 13 metres high and its four corners roughly face the four points of the compass. In the eastern corner, about 1.6 metres from the ground and built into the wall, is a black stone. Tradition claims that this stone fell from heaven and that it was originally white. It then turned black because of people's sin.

The Kiswah

The Kiswah is the black cloth which covers the Ka'aba. A new one is made each year by dedicated craftsmen in Mekkah. It is made of black cloth, which is covered in silk and it has a metre wide band of Arabic text embroidered round it in gold thread. The main part of the text is the Shahadah: 'There is no god but Allah, and Muhammad is the Prophet of Allah', other inscriptions are verses from the Qur'an.

Objectives

Consider the hajj as the fifth pillar of Islam.

Know and understand the nature and importance of the Ka'aba.

Key terms

Hajj: the annual pilgrimage to Makkah, which all Muslims must undertake at least once in their lives, unless prevented by problems over wealth or health. The fifth pillar of Islam.

Pilgrimage: a journey made for religious reasons.

Makkah (Mecca): the city where Muhammad was born. The spiritual centre of Islam; it is in Saudi Arabia.

⚭ links

See the Glossary for a definition of the 'Ka'aba'.

Study tip

You must be able to recognise the Ka'aba from pictures of it.

Discussion activity

Islam teaches that God is everywhere. So why is it necessary for Muslims to go to a special place to worship him?

Research activity

Find out more about the Ka'aba and the black stone set in to its eastern corner from www.sacred-destinations.com/saudi-arabia/mecca-kaba.htm.

For further information on the Kiswah, see 'The making of the Kiswah' on www.islamonline.net. For a quick link to this article, key 'Kiswah' into the search field on the islamonline homepage.

The hajj involves a series of rituals which are carried out in Makkah and in the surrounding area. The main instructions for the hajj are found in the Qur'an but the details are in the sunnah. When they carry out these rituals, Muslims are literally following in the footsteps of the Prophet.

B   Pilgrims from all over the world come to Makkah for the hajj

C   The instructions for hajj are found in the Qur'an

∞ **links**

See the Glossary for a definition of the term 'Ihram'.

Ihram

All pilgrims must wear special clothing. Male Muslims wear Ihram, two sheets of white cloth wrapped around the body. Women must wear clothes of a single colour which cover the whole body, but they do not cover their faces. The clothes show the unity between Muslims regardless of their race or language. They are also a sign of purity and dedication to God. After death, those Muslims who have completed the hajj will be buried in these sheets. Pilgrims put on the Ihram before they approach Makkah and will wear it until the pilgrimage is complete.

Summary

You should now understand that when Muslims go on a pilgrimage to Makkah, they are following in the footsteps of the Prophet. You should also know of the nature and importance of the Ka'aba.

D   Pilgrims wearing Ihram

The rituals of the hajj

Most pilgrims arrive by charter flight and will have changed into their Ihram before they step off the plane. They make their way to Makkah for the first of the rituals. For many, this is an experience they have looked forward to all their life. The **rituals** and **customs** associated with the hajj are very important.

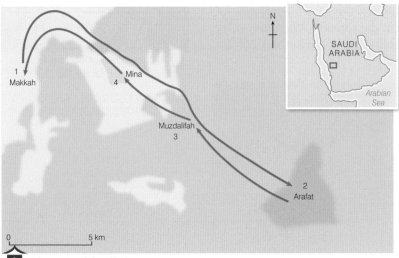

A *The route of the pilgrimage*

1 Makkah

The great crowds of pilgrims must circle the Ka'aba seven times in an anticlockwise direction reciting the pilgrim's prayer as they go. 'Here I am. Oh Lord, at your service. Praise and blessings to you.' To follow the example of the Prophet exactly, each pilgrim must touch the black stone as they pass, or raise their hand to greet it. The crowd then moves on to the covered walkway that links the two small hills of Safa and Marwah. They complete seven circuits between the two points, walking as quickly as the crowd allows. Finally, they return to the Ka'aba to collect water from the well of Zamzam, which is provided in bottles. The pilgrims must then prepare for the 13 mile walk to **Arafat**. High temperatures can make this very difficult, especially for Muslims from colder countries.

2 Arafat

All the pilgrims have to meet at Arafat on the ninth day of the month to perform Wuquf, the ceremony of standing. If they fail to get there in time then they will have to repeat the pilgrimage another year. This is where the Prophet delivered his last sermon. Here the pilgrims join together for prayer and listen to a sermon which is broadcast on loudspeakers and on the radio so that everyone can hear. Much of the day is simply spent in private prayer and thought. This is a desert area, which is intensely hot and dry. A whole city of tents is set up by the authorities, with cooking areas, water supplies and toilets, just for this one day of the year.

B   *Pilgrims during the standing at Arafat*

3 Muzdalifah

The journey to Mina is broken at **Muzdalifah**. On their way the pilgrims must collect 49 small pebbles or stones that will be used in the next ritual. In the past they had to find these small stones themselves, but in 2008, for the first time, they were given them pre-packed in plastic bags. Much of this journey takes place at night. Many of the pilgrims are exhausted by heat and lack of sleep, but they keep going.

C   *A Muslim pilgrim counts his stones in the valley of Mina*

4 Mina

At **Mina** there are three stone pillars called the Jamarat. They represent evil or temptation. The pilgrims throw their pebbles at them to show that they reject evil. This is followed by the feast of sacrifice or Eid ul Adha, which is also celebrated by Muslims all over the world. Animals are sacrificed on behalf of the pilgrims. Then the meat is frozen or canned so that it can be given to the poor. In the following two days, further stoning of the pillars take place. Then the pilgrims return to Makkah for a final circling of the Ka'aba.

Activities

1   Use everything you have learnt about the hajj pilgrimage, including any research you have done, to create you own hajj route.

2   Give a brief explanation of what happens at each place.

3   You could also create a 'virtual hajj' by adding a commentary to images on a slide show presentation.

D   *Pilgrims shave their hair in a traditional ritual on the first day of Eid ul Adha in the valley of Mina*

∞ links

For more information about Eid ul Adha, see Chapter 3, pages 74–75.

Summary

You should now be able to describe and explain the route of the pilgrimage, and you should know that there is a special ritual to be carried out at each place.

Key terms

Muzdalifah: place where pilgrims hold a night prayer and rest during hajj, after the Stand on Mount Arafat.

Mina: place to be visited on hajj – stoning of pillars.

The significance of the hajj

The hajj contains the lessons of all of the pillars. It is a very public declaration of faith, so partly fulfils the duty of shahadah. It is a journey to the centre point of prayer and, like prayer, it is an exercise in God-consciousness. Like zakah it requires Muslims to spend their money in the service of Allah. Like fasting it is physically challenging and requires Muslims to sacrifice their daily comforts. Someone who has completed the pilgrimage is given the title hajji, for a man, or hajja for a woman.

Objectives

Consider the significance of the hajj rituals and the importance of the hajj.

A A hajji's house in Egypt decorated with symbols of the hajj

B Pilgrims stoning pillars

Remembering Abraham

Four of the rituals of hajj are linked with the story of the prophet Abraham who is seen as a perfect example of a man of true faith. Abraham rejected the idol worship of his time and rebuilt the Ka'aba. He was ready to serve God in any way he could, even if it meant sacrificing his son. Muslims follow his example when they circle the Ka'aba and sacrifice an animal. They stone the three pillars in the same way that Abraham threw stones at the devil that tempted him to disobey God. When they run between the two hills and drink the water of Zamzam, pilgrims remember the story of Abraham's wife Hagar. She searched desperately for water for her young son and God rewarded her search with the gift of the well.

The benefits of doing hajj

- **The hajj refreshes faith by bringing it alive**. Being where the Prophet was, and where many important events in his life happened, can help people to remember his example more clearly.

- **The hajj encourages unity among Muslims**. They all meet as equals no matter what their race, wealth or position in society. When they meet Muslims from other countries, they find out about their lives and any difficulties they face. As a result, projects and special charity appeals may be set up by Muslims from richer countries to help those in need.

- **The hajj reminds Muslims of the example of Abraham** and how he showed true faith. This gives Muslims a role model to follow.

links

See the Glossary for more about 'Abraham' and 'Zamzam'.

Extension activity

Find out more about the story of Abraham from the Qur'an 2:124–136.

- **The hajj strengthens God-consciousness** because the pilgrims focus all the time on the feeling that God is with them and watching them.
- **The hajj can lead to forgiveness for sins.** Islam teaches that God will forgive the sins of those who complete the standing at Arafat but only if the Muslim knows they have done wrong, is determined never to do it again and has, in some way, tried to make up for it.

How doing the hajj can affect pilgrims

Case study

In 1964, a black Muslim named Malcolm X made his hajj. Before he went he had a very negative view of white people, but his experiences on hajj changed everything. This is an extract from his autobiography.

> 66 *There were tens of thousands of pilgrims, from all over the world. They were of all colours, from blue-eyed blonds to black-skinned Africans. But we were all participating in the same ritual, displaying a spirit of unity and brotherhood that my experiences in America had led me to believe never could exist between the white and the non-white…*
>
> *You may be shocked by these words coming from me. But on this pilgrimage, what I have seen, and experienced, has forced me to re-arrange much of my thought-patterns previously held, and to toss aside some of my previous conclusions …*
>
> *During the past eleven days here in the Muslim world, I have eaten from the same plate, drunk from the same glass… – while praying to the same God – with fellow Muslims, whose eyes were the bluest of blue, whose hair was the blondest of blond, and whose skin was the whitest of white. And in the words and in the actions and in the deeds of the 'white' Muslims, I felt the same sincerity that I felt among the black African Muslims of Nigeria, Sudan and Ghana.*
>
> *We were truly all the same (brothers) – because their belief in one God had removed the 'white' from their minds, the 'white' from their behaviour, and the 'white' from their attitude.* 99

Autobiography of Malcolm X (1964) cited in Islam the Natural Way, A W Hamid (1989)

C *A brother to all other Muslims*

D *A sister to all other Muslims*

Summary

You should now understand the significance of the hajj rituals and the importance of the hajj for Muslims. The hajj is a very strong spiritual experience in which there are many lessons for pilgrims.

2.10 The purpose and importance of The Five Pillars

The pillars are a training programme that develops the ideal Muslim character and strengthens Islam. Muslims are commanded by God to carry out these duties and to follow the example of the Prophet in the way in which they do so. The purpose and importance of the pillars can be remembered by spelling out the word RUSH. The pillars:

- **R**emind Muslims about the teaching of Islam;
- **U**nite Muslims and strengthen links between them;
- **S**upport the development of God-consciousness;
- **H**elp Muslims to put God first in everything they do.

Shahadah

This pillar reminds Muslims about the purpose of their life which is to worship God by following the teaching of his messenger. When they declare their faith, they are united with other Muslims as everyone tries to fulfil this purpose and feel closer to God.

Salah

Salah reminds Muslims of their duty to God and that all Muslims are equal. It brings Muslims together and makes them feel that God is watching them at all times. It stops them from making everyday life more important than service to God. This is because ordinary life stops for prayer.

Zakah

Zakah reminds richer Muslims of their duty to the poor and strengthens the feelings of brotherhood among Muslims. It also stops wealthy Muslims from making money more important than God.

Objectives

Consider the purpose and importance of The Five Pillars.

links

For a reminder of what each of The Five Pillars represents, see pages 36–37.

A *Love of money must never replace love of God*

Sawm

Sawm reminds Muslims of the teaching of the Qur'an because the whole Qur'an is recited. It unites them because they are all fasting together and break the fast together. It makes them focus on their faith and stops them from making the desires of the body more important than service to God.

Hajj

The hajj reminds Muslims of Abraham. It brings the international community of Muslims together. It makes them focus on God and teaches the importance of sacrifice.

How important are the pillars?

All the pillars are commanded by God but not all of them are duties for all Muslims. Those who are too ill to fast, or too poor to pay zakah or go on hajj, can still lead a life of total obedience to God. Also, in Shi'ah Islam, those whose lives would be in danger if they declared their faith are allowed to keep quiet about it. That leaves prayer. However, those who cannot do the movements of prayer are excused that duty as well, although they are expected to say the words and focus on God. This means that the importance of the pillars varies from person to person. One way of thinking about this is that since they are meant to make you a better Muslim, the one that would help you most is the one that it most important for you.

Activities

These activities consider The Five Pillars.

1. What are Muslims reminded about when they declare their faith?

2. How does salah unite Muslims?

3. 'God expects more from a rich person than he does from a poor person. It's not fair.' What do you think an Imam would say about this view of zakah?

4. 'You only have to fast for a month. You have to pray five times each day.' Which duty do you think is more difficult to do? Give reasons for your answer.

5. 'Poorer Muslims have no chance of going on hajj, so the hajj is not important for them in any way.' Do you agree? Give reasons for your answer.

B *The pillars train Muslims to resist temptation*

C *Muslims are expected to follow God, not fashion*

Activity

6. Get together in teams and make up questions about the pillars with one-word answers. You could use these questions as an end of topic quiz or as crossword clues, or you could make them into a word-search.

Summary

You should now understand the purpose and importance of The Five Pillars. The Pillars RUSH: **R**emind; **U**nite; **S**upport and **H**elp. They are all important because they are commanded by God. However, those who cannot do them can still be good Muslims.

Study tip

Half the marks on the examination paper will be awarded for your ability to express personal opinions or evaluate statements using evidence and argument. This is a skill that needs to be practised.

2

The Five Pillars of Islam – summary

For the examination, you should be able to:

✓ know and understand Muslim attitudes to The Five Pillars

✓ recall and explain what the shahadah is, including the concepts of the Oneness of God and prophethood

✓ explain the practice of salah and consider the importance of prayer in Islam

✓ understand the meaning and importance of:

– the call to prayer

– wudu and rak'ahs

– Jumuah and du'a prayers

✓ explain the practice of zakah and consider its importance

✓ explain the practice of sawm (fasting) in the month of Ramadan and consider its importance

✓ explain the practice of hajj and consider its importance

✓ recall what happens at each of the sites of pilgrimage: Makkah, Arafat, Muzdalifah and Mina, and understand the meaning and importance of these rituals and customs.

Sample answer

1 Write an answer to the following examination question:

'For Muslims, prayer is more important than pilgrimage.' What do you think? Explain your answer.   (*3 marks*)

2 Read the following sample answer:

> Prayer is more important than pilgrimage because Muslims pray every day, but they only have to go on pilgrimage once. Muslims believe that if you stop praying, you will lose your faith in God and stop being a Muslim so it is very important. Muslims have to pray, but they don't have to do pilgrimage if they are sick or poor.

3 With a partner, discuss the sample answer. 3 marks would be awarded for an answer supported by one well developed reason or several simple reasons. Do you think this answer could be improved? If so, how?

4 What mark would you give this answer out of 3? Look at the mark scheme in the Introduction on page 7 (AO2). What are the reasons for the mark you have given?

Practice questions

1   Look at the photograph below and answer the following questions.

(a)   Explain why the Ka'aba is important to Muslims.   *(4 marks)*

(b)   Describe what Muslims do when they go to the Ka'aba on pilgrimage.   *(4 marks)*

> **Study tip**   Make sure you read the question carefully and keep your answer focused. Note it is not asking you what Muslims do at all the sites of pilgrimage, only what they do at the Ka'aba.

(c)   'Muslims do not need a special place in which to worship God.'
Do you agree? Give reasons for your answer, showing that you have thought about more than one point of view.   *(6 marks)*

> **Study tip**   You can use information from more than one topic to help you answer any questions you are asked. In this question, a 'special place' could be a mosque or the Ka'aba, or any of the other pilgrimage sites.

(d)   Explain how Muslims carry out the duty of fasting in the month of Ramadan.   *(4 marks)*

(e)   'God knows everything, so there is no point in praying to him.'
Do you agree? Give reasons for your answer, showing that you have thought about more than one point of view. Refer to Islam in your answer.   *(6 marks)*

3 Worship

3.1 The mosque: exterior design

The mosque

Beliefs and teachings

Whoever builds a mosque for Allah, Allah will build for him a house in Paradise.

Hadith

A **mosque** is the Muslim place of prayer. It is very likely that wherever you are in the UK, there is a mosque not far from you. If the local Muslim community is small, the mosque may be only a room set aside for prayer. Often the mosque is a converted house where daily prayers are held. Purpose-built mosques can be found in towns and cities, like Birmingham, which have large Muslim populations. These will hold many worshippers and provide all the facilities needed for prayer, and often much more. The UK national mosque is in Regent's Park, London. It was designed to hold 4500 people for prayer, and in summer another 1000 people can worship in its open-air forecourt.

Mosque design

The Qur'an does not mention what a mosque should look like so there are many different styles around the world. However, they share many features. They are all positioned so that those using the prayer hall will be facing Makkah. Some are easy to recognise because they have a dome and one or more towers called minarets. The Islamic symbol of the crescent moon and star often appears on the top of the minaret or dome, and the stonework itself may be decorated with Arabic script.

Objectives

Recall and explain what a mosque is.

Identify the main external features of a mosque and explain their significance.

Key terms

Mosque: a Muslim place of worship.

A *Birmingham Central Mosque*

B *A minaret*

C *The crescent moon and star*

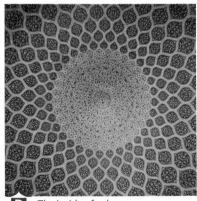

D *The inside of a dome*

Minaret and dome

In the past, the minaret was used by the mu'adhin who would call Muslims to prayer from the top of the tower. Now it is often purely decorative. In some countries it contains the loudspeakers through which the call to prayer is played. The dome sits above the prayer hall. It is said to represent the universe and to remind Muslims that the whole world belongs to God. Its design helps the sound of the prayer to carry all round the prayer hall and to keep the room cool. It is often beautifully decorated, both inside and out. When a mosque has four minarets and a dome, these are said to symbolise The Five Pillars of Islam.

E *A mosque dome from outside*

Rooms for ritual washing

Mosques need somewhere for worshippers to perform wudu. This can be a courtyard fountain or special ablution rooms near the prayer hall. Large mosques which hold many people need very large rooms. This is because everyone needs to perform wudu at the same time. The Hassan II Mosque in Morocco can hold up to 25,000 worshippers inside and up to 80,000 outside. It has two large rooms, one for women and another for men, built beneath the mosque.

F *The ritual washing rooms, Great Mosque Hassan II, Casablanca, Morocco*

Summary

You should now be able to describe the outside of a mosque, identify the main external features and explain their significance.

links

For more information about the mu'adhin and the call to prayer, see pages 64–65.

Extension activity

Use the internet to find out more about the Blue Mosque in Turkey.

Non-Muslim tourists often visit this mosque. Find out what they must do as they enter and what they would see. Do you think holy buildings should be tourist sites?

links

Take a virtual tour of one British mosque. For example, visit the following website and follow the Discovery link to take a virtual tour of the mosque: **www.lancashiremosques.com**

Activity

To learn the main features of a mosque, create a flashcard for each one. You will need a piece of paper or card at least the size of a playing card. On the first, write 'dome' on one side, or draw a picture of a dome. On the other side of the card you can write the details of what it is and what it does or is used for. Make other cards for the minaret and the ablution room or fountain. You will make more cards as you go through the chapter.

links

For more information about wudu and ritual washing, see Chapter 2, pages 40–41.

Study tip

In your examination you may be given colour pictures to use as a starting point for your answers. Make sure you can recognise the main features of a mosque from their pictures.

The mosque is the heart of the Muslim community and the prayer hall is the heart of the mosque. Males and females may enter the hall through separate doors. They will pray in different parts of the room, or have separate prayer rooms, so that they do not distract each other. Everything in the prayer hall is designed to create the right atmosphere for prayer. Prayers can only be performed in a clean place so it is important that the prayer hall is kept dirt-free. Just outside the prayer hall will be a place where everyone can leave their shoes before entering. This has to be carefully organised in a large mosque because as many as 25,000 people could be trying to find their shoes at the end of the prayers.

▇ Qiblah and mihrab

The direction of prayer or **qiblah** will be shown by an alcove or niche called a **mihrab**. All Muslims have to face the Sacred Mosque at Makkah when they pray. Makkah is south-east from the UK so this is the qiblah, the direction of prayer. When Muslims focus on one single point in prayer, they are reminded that their lives should focus only on God. They also feel that they are part of a large worldwide community. This is because all Muslims, no matter where they are, focus on that one single point for prayer. The mihrab may be highly decorated but it may also be very simple so as not to distract the worshipper.

Objectives

Identify the main features of a prayer hall and understand their use.

Key terms

Qiblah: the direction of Makkah.

Mihrab: a niche indicating the direction of Makkah.

Minbar: a pulpit for giving Friday sermons.

Study tip

Make sure you can explain the terms qiblah, mihrab and minbar, and use them in your answers in the examination.

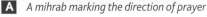

A   *A mihrab marking the direction of prayer*

B   *A minbar*

▇ Minbar

When the Imam delivers his sermon, he will stand on a **minbar** which will be on the same wall as the alcove. This may be a very simple set of steps or a very ornate feature. Its purpose is simply to allow the congregation to see and hear the preacher.

⬭⬭ links

You will learn more about the Imam on pages 66–67.

The prayer hall, like the rest of the mosque, will have no pictures or statues in it. Muslims believe that God cannot be represented in any form because he is unique. They totally reject the worship of images because only God should be worshipped. Instead, verses from the Qur'an, or the shahadah, decorate the walls and the inside of the dome. Geometric patterns may also be used.

Extension activity

Use the internet to find out more about Arabic calligraphy. Use illustrations you find there to design a poster illustrating this form of Islamic art.

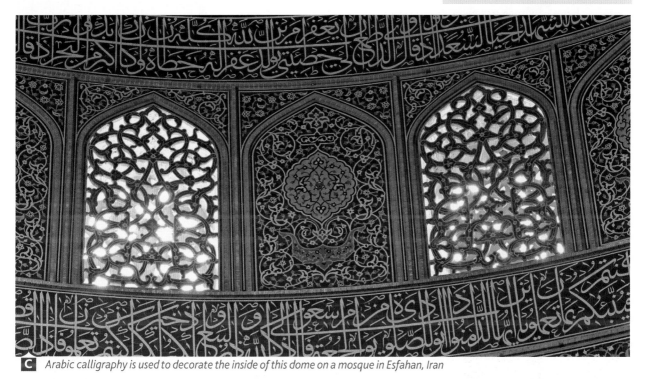

C   *Arabic calligraphy is used to decorate the inside of this dome on a mosque in Esfahan, Iran*

The prayer carpet may have a pattern that marks out the space for each person to pray. It is laid so that the worshippers are facing Makkah in rows. Sometimes individual prayer mats are used. On one wall of the room there is often a clock display showing the times of the five daily prayers and of the Friday Jumuah prayer.

D   *Prayer carpet. Its design helps people to organise themselves for prayer*

links

For more information about the Friday Jumuah prayer, see Chapter 2, pages 42–43.

Research activity

Research the various designs that are used for a prayer mat or carpet.

Activity

Design five more flashcards to represent: qiblah, mihrab, minbar, carpet and clocks. Write carefully on the back of each one what the item is and how it is used.

Summary

You should now be able to identify the main features of a prayer hall, and understand their use.

A Muslim man praying on a prayer mat

■ Compass and prayer mat

Muslims can turn any suitable place into a mosque by using a compass and a prayer mat. The compass is used to work out the direction of prayer. Today Muslims can use small electronic gadgets and satellite data to tell them where Makkah is in relation to where they are. The prayer mat is used to make sure the place of prayer is clean. Each mat is about a metre long and half a metre wide. The colourful decoration will include an arch which the worshipper will point in the direction of Makkah. There is often a deliberate mistake in the pattern. This is to remind Muslims that only God is perfect.

Objectives

Identify aids to worship and understand their use.

B Electronic qiblah direction finder

∞ links

See page 60 for a reminder of what 'qiblah' means.

Case study

Taking time out for prayer

The meeting had been full of lively discussion for a few hours and we were all more than ready to eat. As we broke up for lunch, most people moved off quickly to the restaurant but one man stayed behind. He picked up his briefcase, opened it, and took out a rolled up mat and a small electronic device into which he punched some numbers. (I found out later that it was the postcode for the building we were in.) He checked the display and then went over to the corner of the room carrying the mat. He checked the device again and then carefully placed the mat down. A moment later he began to pray.

C A qiblah compass

Activities

1 Look at Photo **A** of the Muslim man praying. Why is he using a prayer mat and why did he need a compass to make sure that the prayer mat was in the right position?

2 Read the case study, and answer the following questions. Make sure you explain each of your answers.

a Do you think the Muslim found it easy to pray in this situation?

b How do you think the people who saw him pray felt about what he was doing?

Study tip

In the examination, you will be asked for your opinion and told to explain your answer. The marks for such questions are for the explanation you give, not your point of view.

■ Qur'an stand

All copies of the Qur'an must always be treated with great respect because they contain the words of God as given directly to the Prophet. Muslims will always wash their hands before touching a Qur'an. Also, stands are used to make sure that the Qur'an never touches an unclean surface or the ground. The stand is also called a throne. Muslims reciting or studying the Qur'an will sit on the floor and put the Qur'an on its stand in front of them so that they can read it.

■ Prayer beads

Prayer beads are used by some Muslims in private prayer to help them count when they recite the names of God. They move one bead along the string each time they say a name. Many strings have 99 beads, one for each of God's names; some have 33 in which case Muslims go round the string three times. This aid helps Muslims to concentrate on their prayers.

D *Prayer beads*

E *A Qur'an stand*

F *Muslims do not have to pray in a special building. Muhammad said, 'The whole world has been made a place of prostration.'*

Summary

You should now be able to identify various Muslim aids to worship and understand their use.

Research activity 🔍

Find out more about how Muslims treat the Qur'an with respect, and what they do with old copies of the Qur'an once they are no longer needed for study or worship.

Discussion activity 👥

Read each of the following statements:

- Aids to worship like these are not necessary.
- Muslims can pray anywhere, so special buildings are not needed.
- You cannot be a good Muslim if you never go to a mosque.

What do you think? Explain your opinion.

Read the Study tip before you start.

Activity

3 Create flashcards for each of the items mentioned: prayer mat, compass, prayer beads and Qur'an stand. You should now have 12 cards. Use them to test each other.

Mu'adhin

The **mu'adhin (muezzin)** is the person who calls Muslims to prayer and the **adhan** is the call to prayer itself. The only qualifications needed to be a mu'adhin are to be a good Muslim man with a strong voice. In Muhammad's time, the mu'adhin would walk though the streets of the city to call the faithful to prayer. After mosques were built he would call from the top of the minaret. In many Muslim countries today the voice of the mu'adhin is amplified by speakers. This means that, no matter what time of day or how busy the streets are, people can hear the call. In non-Muslim countries, the adhan is usually called inside the mosque. The mu'adhin may become a local or national celebrity. Recordings from popular mu'adhins are broadcast on the radio at prayer times or used in adhan alarm clocks like the one pictured in Photo **C**. Recordings may also be used as ringtones on mobile phones which are set to go off when prayer times arrive. Turkey holds an annual competition to find the best mu'adhin.

Objectives

Know and understand the role of the mu'adhin and the use and significance of the adhan.

Key terms

Mu'adhin (muezzin): the Islamic call to prayer (the person who calls).

Adhan: the call to prayer.

Study tip

Do not get the mu'adhin and the adhan mixed up. Remembering that 'm' is for both 'man' and 'mu'adhin' might help.

A   *Adhan competition in Turkey*

Extension activity

Write an advert for a new mu'adhin (muezzin). You will need to explain what the role involves and what qualifications the person needs.

Adhan

The Arabic words of the adhan itself are a reminder of some of the most important truths of Islam. They also remind Muslims that they should stop whatever they are doing to make time for prayer. We can see this in the call for the pre-dawn prayer which includes an extra phrase, the words 'prayer is better than sleep'. Any visiting traveller will know that they are in a Muslim country when they hear the adhan; it is a sign of the people's faith.

B   *Cairo skyline*

The mu'adhin in action

4.30am, Cairo, Egypt. As in other Muslim countries, in the silence of the early morning before dawn, a single voice starts in the distance. Rising and falling with repeated phrases, it begins to echo around the town. It is picked up by other voices from left and right, near and far, until the whole sky is full of sound. In the UK, the same sound comes from an alarm clock at the side of a sleeping Muslim waking her with a start. She gets out of bed and goes to the bathroom to perform wudu, then offers the first prayers of the day.

Beliefs and teachings

The Adhan

God is most great, God is most great.	Allahu Akbar, Allahu Akbar.
I testify that there is no god but God.	Ashhadu an la ilaha ill-Allah.
I testify that there is no god but God.	Ashhadu an la ilaha ill-Allah.
I testify that Muhammad is the Prophet of God.	Ashhadu anna Muhammad ar Rasoolullah.
I testify that Muhammad is the Prophet of God.	Ashhadu anna Muhammad ar Rasoolullah.
Come to prayer, come to prayer.	Hayya 'alas-Salah. Hayya 'alas-Salah.
Come to salvation, come to salvation.	Hayya 'alal-falah. Hayya 'alal-falah.
God is most great, God is most great.	Allahu Akbar. Allahu Akbar.
There is no god but God.	La ilaha ill-Allah.

The adhan is not just used to call to prayer; it is also spoken into the ear of a newborn child so that one of the first sounds the child hears is the call to worship God. It is also often the first thing said when Muslims move into a new house that they are about to make into their home.

∞ links

You can hear the adhan for yourself at **www.audioquraan.com**
On this website you will find a direct link to various adhans around the world.

Discussion activity

With a partner, discuss whether Muslims should be allowed to broadcast the call to prayer from mosques in Britain. Give your reasons, and be prepared to discuss your ideas with the class.

Activities

1   Find **three** key Muslim beliefs in the adhan and write them down.
2   Write each of the lines of the adhan on a separate strip of paper and mix them up. Without looking at the book, try to put them in order.

Summary

You should now know and understand the role of the mu'adhin, and the use and significance of the adhan.

C   *Automatic adhan clock*

The role of the Imam

The title **Imam** means 'prayer leader'. If two or more Muslims are praying together, one will be chosen to act as the Imam. When a family prays together the father will be the Imam, he will face the qiblah and the family will take their places behind him.

Today the title of Imam is used for the leader of the mosque employed by the mosque committee. He will lead the prayers, preach the Friday sermon, conduct funerals and provide guidance and advice on all matters of Muslim belief and behaviour. An Imam will also teach Arabic and Qur'an recitation and study. This gives the Imam a lot of influence in the mosque.

A Here the man is acting as Imam for the woman

Qualities of an Imam

An **Imam** will be someone respected by the people both for his views and for the way in which he leads his life. He will be an expert on the Qur'an and its meaning and on the teaching of Islam. He will be wise in his understanding of how that teaching can apply to modern situations. It is also important that an Imam is a good speaker. Some British mosques have non-English-speaking Imams. Many Muslims, however, believe that it is important that Imams in Britain should speak English and understand the British way of life. This is so that they can present Islam to non-Muslims and talk directly to young people and understand their situation.

C London central Mosque

Objectives

Know and be able to explain the role of the Imam.

Key terms

Imam: a person who leads communal prayer.

B The Imams not only provide guidance to visitors to the mosque, many also answer questions online

Research activity

Investigate the services offered by the Imams based at the London Central Mosque by visiting the religious services section of its website: www.iccuk.org

Young Muslims have to be encouraged to go to the mosque but they often understand English only and they are easily bored. It is important for the Imam to make his talks and presentations interesting for them, both in what he says and how he puts it over.

The Imam, with the backing of the mosque committee, can make the mosque an important centre for all Muslims in the community. In 2008, the North London Central Mosque was voted 'Best European Islamic Centre' by readers of the website Islamonline.net. It runs activities in many different languages including Arabic, English, Somali, Kurdish, Urdu, Bengali and Albanian, to meet the needs of the many different nationalities that live in the area. It offers a wide range of courses from literacy and IT classes to keep-fit, and from classes in maths and science to classes in Qur'an study.

D *Imam Ahmed Sa'd of the North London Central Mosque*

Discussion activity

Should women be able to be Imans in mixed congregations?

◼ Can the Imam be a woman?

Islam has always allowed a woman to be the Imam when no men are present. However, most Muslims believe that when the congregation is mixed, the Imam must be a man. In October 2008 a woman, Professor Amina Wadud, was invited to lead Friday prayers for a congregation of both men and women, at the Muslim Education Centre, Oxford. This was the first time a woman had led Friday prayers in the UK, and not everyone approved. The organisers were sure that she had the right qualities because of her knowledge and understanding of the Qur'an. The person chosen to be the Imam for any prayer should be the best informed about the Qur'an and Islam.

Study tip

You are asked to study the role of the Imam, and must recognise the word 'role' if the examiners use it.

The Imam has a part to play during prayers, in the mosque and in the community. This is their role.

Activity

1   A mosque needs to appoint a new Imam. Imagine that you are writing the job description for the position.

a   What would you expect the Imam to do, and what type of character or personality should the Imam have?

b   Would you allow women to apply?

Summary

You should now understand and be able to explain that the role of the Imam is to lead communal prayer.

Many mosques are far more than places of worship. A modern purpose-built mosque may offer many facilities and services for the community.

■ Education

Many mosques run a **madrassah** or school. Here children can learn Arabic and how to recite the Qur'an. They are also taught how to be a good Muslim. Their Islamic education can include the basics of cleanliness, good morals and good manners as well as basic knowledge about beliefs and practices. This is vitally important because such education is not normally available in local state schools. Each new generation has to be taught Islam so that it can pass it on to the next. Parents are expected to do more than just send their children to the madrassah. They should also be setting a good example for the child by living a Muslim life.

The madrassah also runs Qur'an study groups for adults, often with separate classes for women and men. A library, reading rooms and bookshops support those attending the madrassah and may also provide information for non-Muslims visiting the mosque.

■ Social events and funerals

Mosques often have kitchens where food can be prepared and large meeting rooms which can be used for festivals and for family celebrations after weddings and naming ceremonies.

Many also have a mortuary where the body is prepared for burial. For example, the Hendon Mosque and Islamic Centre offers a complete funeral service.

The mosque has a fully-equipped vehicle on standby to collect the body after death. They can usually carry out burials on the same day, in almost any local cemetery, as long as the legal formalities are complete. The mosque provides a full service for men and women that complies with the Shari'ah law.

The standard service includes:

- the final bathing of the deceased;
- the shrouding of the deceased;
- 48-hour use of the mortuary where the body will be kept if necessary;
- supply of a suitable coffin or casket;
- transport for the deceased;
- the Imam's services on request.

■ The mosque and the wider community

A purpose-built mosque is a very public statement about what Islam is and what it stands for. The worshippers who go to the mosque are expected to act as representatives for Islam. They also have a duty to introduce others to Islam by informing them about its teachings

Key terms

Madrassah: a Muslim school attached to a mosque where young Muslims study Islam.

A *Learning to write in Arabic*

∞ links

For further details of the funeral service offered by the Hendon Mosque and Islamic Centre, visit their website at:
www.hendonmosque.co.uk

Research activity

1 Find out more about Muslim funeral customs.

and practices. Many mosques invite non-Muslim visitors and provide visiting speakers for schools, radio or television. They may host websites and some broadcast radio programmes, especially during the month of Ramadan. Muslim Community Radio in East London provides children's shows, quizzes, prayer sessions, chat shows and Qur'an classes both in English and in Bangla, the language of Bangladeshi Muslims.

B   *An example of a programme of events run by a mosque*

Mon	Tue	Weds	Thurs	Fri	Sat	Sun
Ladies Qur'an classes 10–12	Men's Qur'an classes 6–8	Women's group for senior citizens 10–1	Keep fit 6–8	Boys' youth club 7–9.30	Girls' Urdu 10.30–12 Boys' youth club 2–4	Study group for new Muslims 11–1.30

Services provided by Birmingham Central Mosque:

- marriage bureau & introductions;
- family support service & counselling clinic;
- Shari'ah council;
- funerals;
- Islam embracing service for those interested in committing themselves to Islam.

Research activity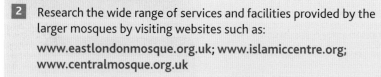

2   Research the wide range of services and facilities provided by the larger mosques by visiting websites such as:

www.eastlondonmosque.org.uk; www.islamiccentre.org; www.centralmosque.org.uk

C   *Students learning to study and recite the Qur'an at a madrassah*

links

See Chapter 5 for more information about how the mosque supports family life.

Activities

1   Make a spider diagram showing all the different activities that may take place in a mosque. You may want to use the website of one of the mosques mentioned on this page to help you.

2   Explain how the mosque helps to educate young Muslims.

3   Give **two** other services the mosque provides for the Muslim community.

4   Explain how the mosque helps non-Muslims to find out about Islam.

Summary

You should now understand the role of the mosque in the community, that it is a centre of worship, a centre of education, and the focus and heart of community life.

Study tip

Make sure that you learn examples of the different services that mosques provide so that you can explain your answers fully.

Is a mosque important?

Try to imagine what a Muslim community in Britain would lose if it had no mosque. It would have no central meeting place and nowhere the whole community could get together for prayers. New Muslims moving into the area would not know where to go to meet up with other Muslims and there would be nowhere to go for advice or for a Muslim education. You may be able to think of other ways in which the community would miss the mosque. All this suggests that it is extremely important for a Muslim community to have a mosque.

Look again at what the mosque does for Muslims. How much could be done online in a virtual mosque? There are already online advice forums like 'Ask the Imam' and social networking sites allow Muslims to exchange information. Mobile phones let people talk to each other – you don't have to meet. Is the online mosque the mosque of the future?

Objectives

Consider differing views about the importance of the mosque.

A   *The dome of this modern mosque in Birmingham is a local landmark for muslims living in the area*

Activities

1   Read the following statements about the mosque:
- Mosques can attract non-believers to Islam by showing Islam exists, making them curious about it, and giving them an opportunity to find out more.
- Mosques are too small for Eid prayers.
- Mosques are a meeting place for the community and a centre of worship and education.
- No one has to go to a mosque to pray.
- The services and facilities of a mosque are used by many Muslims.
- God tells wives and mothers that doing their duty to their family is more important than going to the mosque to pray.

2   Now do the following:
a   Choose and write down **two** of these statements which can be used as evidence that the mosque is **not** important in Islam.
b   Choose and write down **two** statements which could be used as evidence that the mosque **is** important in Islam.
c   Are there any other arguments for either opinion which are not included here?
d   Which side of the argument is the stronger?
e   Are mosques important or are they not?

Study tip

Always expect to find different opinions in any debate. Practise finding the evidence and argument for more than one point of view.

Extension activity

Imagine the local Muslim community planned to set up a virtual mosque. Think about what it would need to include and what advantages there could be in having one. Then design an online advert for your virtual mosque.

If mosques are important, the next questions are: how much should a Muslim community spend on building a mosque? What facilities should it include? How ornate and decorative should it be? The earliest mosques were modelled on the one built by Muhammad and his followers in Madinah. This was a simple courtyard alongside his house which provided some shade for people at prayer and was also used as a meeting place. Simple steps were used as a minbar so that everyone

B *This magnificent new mosque in Abu Dhabi was opened in 2007*

could see Muhammad when he delivered a sermon, and the call to prayer was given from the roof. Today, in contrast, many mosques are magnificent, expensive buildings intended to show the greatness of God. Islam teaches that people should not waste the resources God has given them, so should so much money be spent on a building when it could be used to support poorer Muslims instead?

C *A mosque made of mud in the Mali village of Telei*

Conclusions

Some mosques are very important. The Great Mosque in Makkah is an international symbol of Islam and the focus of every prayer. Many Muslims see the larger British mosques as the centre of the community and a visual reminder of their duty to God. Some Muslims do not go to the mosque very often. They use their homes, work or schools as places of prayer, keep in touch with others by phone or email, and learn about Islam from the internet or books.

Summary

You should now be aware of differing views about the importance of the mosque. While mosques are very important for some Muslims, it is possible for Muslims to worship God without mosques.

D *Should the money spent on mosques be used instead to improve the life of beggars like this?*

3.8 Eid ul Fitr

Eid ul Fitr starts as Ramadan ends. It celebrates the 'breaking of the fast', the end of the very strict discipline of fasting in daylight hours. The Eid prayer is held outside, weather permitting, to allow as many people as possible to pray together. Everyone wears their best clothes and many buy new clothes for the occasion. On their way to the Eid prayer, the crowds repeatedly chant Allahu Akbar (God is great).

Objectives

Describe how Eid ul Fitr is celebrated.

Key terms

Eid ul Fitr: celebration of the end of fasting after Ramadan.

Dates for Eid ul Fitr

2009:	20 September
2010:	10 September
2011:	29 August
2012:	18 August
2013:	7 August
2014:	28 July

Research activity

Find out how the date for Eid ul Fitr is decided.

A   *Festive open air prayers for Indonesian women on Eid ul Fitr*

The Imam's sermon, during this festival, reminds Muslims that it is their duty to care for all living beings, end hatred and anger, and help the poor and needy. Muslims should go away from the sermon wanting to end suffering and unfairness wherever they find it. When the Imam announces the start of the celebration, everyone greets and hugs those around them and then visits their family and friends to share cards, presents and a celebration meal. There is a great community spirit and no one is left out. Muslims are expected to give a special payment to charity (Zakah ul fitr), in thankfulness that they have been able to fast during Ramadan. This payment will be given before the Eid celebrations begin. Some of this money will be spent on making sure that the poor can also join in the celebrations. Even the dead are not forgotten, as many people will go to the graves of the dead to show respect.

B   *Sweets are a popular part of the Eid celebrations*

Eid ul Fitr around the world

The way Eid ul Fitr is celebrated varies over the Muslim world, but almost everywhere food plays an important part and special dishes are prepared for the occasion. In Malaysia, there are three days of public holidays and celebrations go on for a whole month. Their special dishes include rice cooked in coconut leaves or bamboo shoots and served with beef. In Iraq, a special breakfast of buffalo cream with honey and bread is eaten, while in Egypt, where there are four days of celebration, the festive meal is fish based.

C   *The festive Malaysian dish of rice cooked in banana skin*

Case study

Eid ul Fitr in one Manchester family

The night before Eid, we all go out to the shops in Manchester, which are open late, and take the kids along. Everyone is rushing around buying clothes, food and sweets from their favourite sweet shop. We all get lovely new clothes, even the baby! When we finally get home from the shops, my youngest sister and I decorate our hands, and the children's hands, with henna.

On the morning of Eid we all wake very early and eat delicious, traditional sweet vermicelli (fine noodles) cooked in milk with nuts and cardamom, all of us saying 'Eid Mubarak!' (blessed festival) and hugging and kissing. The girls love it and always ask for second helpings. My husband goes to the mosque while I, my sister and the children, stay at home to pray. Then we visit lots of friends living nearby. Afterwards we go home, our family comes over and the children get their gifts at last. When I was small we used to get Eidi, which is a traditional gift of money, but now the girls get presents. This year they got the dolls they had wished for.

My husband's family and my sister then come round for Eid lunch, which is a huge feast. Everyone is always very happy and excited to be eating lovely food again! We also invite others from the mosque, who might not have family here and may be feeling lonely. We eat spicy rice with meat, chicken curry, lamb kebabs, rasmalai (sweet milky dishes), mithai (sweets), kheer (sweet rice dessert) and Eid cakes. All the kids run around and eat too many sweets.

Adapted from http://www.yourfamily.org.uk

Extension activity

Design a card for Eid ul Fitr. Make sure your card sums up what Eid ul Fitr means for Muslims. You will find many examples online. You could make your card an e-card.

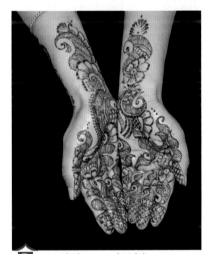

D   *Hands decorated with henna*

Activities

1   What are the three teachings given by the Imam in his Eid ul Fitr sermon?

2   Using evidence from the case study, find three different ways in which Muslim families celebrate Eid ul Fitr.

3   Explain how the community makes sure no one is left out of the celebrations.

Summary

You should now be able to describe how Eid ul Fitr is celebrated, and you should know that this celebration takes place at the end of fasting after Ramadan.

Study tip

Make sure you always read questions carefully and do exactly what the question asks you to do.

3.9 Eid ul Adha

Eid ul Adha is the feast of sacrifice celebrated by pilgrims on hajj and by Muslims worldwide. The festival falls towards the end of the hajj in the last month of the year on the Islamic calendar. It celebrates how the prophet Ibrahim was willing to sacrifice his son for God. On the day itself, there are congregational prayers in the mosque. So many people want to attend these prayers that they are repeated many times. That way everyone gets a chance to take part. In Muslim countries the Eid is a public holiday but in Britain people need to ask for time off work or school. Despite this, the number of people who take part is impressive. For example, up to 50,000 people go to the national mosque in London for the Eid prayers.

Dates for Eid ul Adha	
2009:	28 November
2010:	17 November
2011:	7 November
2012:	26 October
2013:	15 October
2014:	4 October

A Mosques are full for Eid prayers

The festival is a time for celebration. Muslims who are away from home come back to visit family and friends and to share festive meals. Everyone sends cards and gives presents. Community celebrations are often organised. These can include such things as a funfair, games, sports, entertainment, talks and displays, a bazaar, competitions and fireworks. There may be separate celebrations for men and women. The festivities can go on for up to four days. Care is taken to make sure that no one is left out of the celebrations. People living on their own are invited to share meals with their neighbours, and anyone who is in hospital can be sure of having plenty of visitors.

■ Animal sacrifice

Animal sacrifice plays an important part in the celebration of Eid ul Adha. However, some Muslims believe that it is only a duty for those doing the pilgrimage.

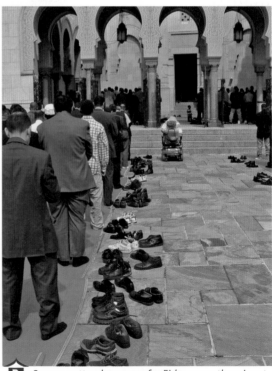

B So many attend mosques for Eid prayers, there is not room for all of them inside

Farmers bring their animals to Makkah to sell and to make sure that there will be one for anyone who wants to make the sacrifice. Enormous freezers are provided so that the meat will not be wasted. This is a huge and costly operation, for which pilgrims are charged around £100. Male pilgrims will perform the sacrifice on behalf of their family, or pay for someone else to do it if they think they will not be able to do it painlessly. The animal is killed in the way laid down by Islamic law, so that its meat is halal. One third of the meat is given to the poor, one third to family and friends, and the rest is eaten during the festival. The sacrifice is widely practised in other countries too but some Muslims choose to give money instead. British law forbids Muslims from killing an animal themselves. Some British Muslims will buy an animal which is then killed on their behalf at a local slaughterhouse. Others make a sacrifice of money which is used to support other Muslims.

Beliefs and teachings

The animal offerings are among the rites decreed by God for your own good (for hajj). You shall mention God's name on them while they are standing in line. Once they are offered for sacrifice, you shall eat from them and feed the poor and the needy.
Qur'an 22:36

C *In countries like Pakistan, animals are given garlands to wear before they are sacrificed*

Eid ul Adha is sometimes called the Offer Feast because of the offering Muslins make to God. In some countries special arrangements are made for the killing of so many animals on one day. Belgium, for example, sets up special slaughterhouses just for the occassion. One French supermarket buys the meat of animals sacrificed for Eid so that Muslims can then buy that meat instead of sacrificing an animal themselves. The arrangement is approved by Muslim leaders, but not all Muslims are happy with it because they feel that the example of the Prophet is not being completely followed.

⊖⊖links

See Chapter 4, pages 84–85, for more information about halal and the way in which animals are sacrificed for food.

Study tip

Take care to read the whole of the question. If you do not refer to Islam in your answer, you will not be able to gain full marks.

Activities

1 Using the information on this page, explain how Eid ul Adha is celebrated in the mosque and in the home.

2 'Festivals are mostly for children.' What do you think? Explain your opinion. Refer to Islam in your answer.

Read the Study tip before you tackle the second activity.

Summary

You should now be able to describe how Eid ul Adha is celebrated in the mosque, the family and the community.

Both Eid ul Fitr and Eid ul Adha are great social occasions with feasting, presents, parties and cards. In some areas, excited groups of mostly younger Muslims will get together and roads will be closed for lively street parties. Both festivals were celebrated by the Prophet so Muslims celebrating them today are following his example, even if some of the ways in which they celebrate are very modern.

Objectives

Consider the religious significance of Eid ul Fitr and Eid ul Adha.

■ Eid in the Square

A First ever Eid ul Fitr party in Trafalgar Square, London in 2006

This is the celebration of Eid ul Fitr held in Trafalgar Square, London, each year. There is live entertainment, stalls and exhibitions as well as places to meet, eat and celebrate together.

Case study

Eid in Manchester

Every year during Eid, Rusholme (Manchester) is a scene of colour and noise. Muslims from all over the area, many dressed in their best clothes, gather together to celebrate. Some arrive in stretch limos or open top cars – sounding car horns, playing music and waving Pakistani flags. Restaurants are full of happy families, as they welcome family members who live and work away from home. The community leaders and local Imams are also celebrating but they try to keep an eye on the loud and enthusiastic younger Muslims. They do not want their celebrations to annoy other people in the area.

■ Eid ul Fitr

Eid ul Fitr celebrates the end of the fast. While they fast, Muslims are reminded of the sacrifice God expects from them. In contrast, Eid ul Fitr is a celebration of the joy and happiness that are the rewards of obedience to God. At this festival, Muslims are celebrating being Muslims. They celebrate the gifts given to them by God, the gift of the Qur'an and of the food and drink which they need to live. They also celebrate being part of a community in which everyone cares for everyone else. The main themes of Eid ul Fitr are gratitude to God, concern for others, and the pleasure of being a Muslim.

B Iraqi Muslims celebrating in Baghdad. Funfairs are part of the celebrations of both Eids

Eid ul Adha

Part of Eid ul Adha has an obvious religious significance. The sacrifice remembers an event in the life of the prophet Abraham, when he dreamt that he sacrificed his son. He believed that this was what God was asking him to do. The story can be found in Qur'an 37:102–107. After Abraham showed that he was willing to make this great sacrifice, God provided an animal to be sacrificed instead. The Qur'an describes Abraham as a good example to Muslims. He showed that perfect Muslims must obey God in all things and be willing to give up anything if God commands it, even what they love most.

The Qur'an (22:37) tells Muslims that it is not the meat or blood of the animal that they are offering to God. All animals that are to be eaten are killed in the same way, so in that sense the animal sacrifice on Eid ul Adha is nothing special. The real sacrifice is the gift of the meat to friends and the poor. When they offer that, they are following the example of the Prophet and obeying God.

> 66 (We Muslims show) a willingness to make sacrifices in our lives in order to stay on the Straight Path. Each of us makes small sacrifices, giving up things that are fun or important to us. A true Muslim, one who submits his or herself completely to the Lord, is willing to follow Allah's commands completely and obediently. It is this strength of heart, purity in faith, and willing obedience that our Lord desires from us. 99
>
> http://islam.about.com/od/hajj/a/adha.htm

C Livestock market of animals for Muslim festival of sacrifice

Conclusion

Worship in Islam is not just carrying out the special religious duties God has commanded. It also involves living your whole life in obedience to God and following the example of the Prophet. Religion is not just special actions and words at special times and in special places. It is a complete way of life. These festivals celebrate what it means to be a Muslim and to be a member of the Muslim community. They are about belonging. Muslims should love each other as if they were brother and sister. The Eids demand and encourage this and provide an opportunity for that love to be shown.

Study tip

In the examination, you will be given statements like the one in the Activity box, and then asked, 'Do you agree? Give reasons for your answer, showing that you have thought about more than one point of view.'

Activity

Remind yourself of how the two festivals are celebrated in Islam and consider the information presented on this page. Work in pairs. One person must find evidence to support the claim that the festivals are great social events. The other person must find evidence to support the claim that the festivals are important religious events. Then use the evidence to argue for or against the claim: 'The festivals are just times when families can have fun; they have no religious importance.'

Look at the Study tip before you start this activity.

Summary

You should now understand the religious significance of the two Muslim festivals: Eid ul Fitr and Eid ul Adha.

Worship – summary

For the examination, you should be able to:

✔ know and understand how the mosque reflects and affects the style of worship that takes place within it

✔ know and understand the design and functions of a mosque

✔ identify the main features and symbols of a mosque – mihrab, qiblah, minbar – and explain their significance

✔ identify aids to worship and understand their use and importance

✔ understand the role and importance of the Imam

✔ understand the role and importance of the mu'adhin (muezzin)

✔ know and understand the importance of the adhan – the call to prayer

✔ consider the role of the madrassah

✔ describe how Eid ul Fitr and Eid ul Adha are celebrated, and consider their importance for Muslims.

Sample answer

1 Write an answer to the following examination question:

Explain the importance of Eid ul Adha for Muslims.

(6 marks)

2 Read the following sample answer:

> Eid ul Adha is the feast of sacrifice which is celebrated as part of the pilgrimage. Muslims remember how prophet Abraham was willing to sacrifice his son when God commanded him to do it. After Abraham had showed that his faith was strong, and that he would kill his son, God sent an animal and it was killed instead. This shows what being a Muslim is all about, you must be able to make sacrifices for God.

3 With a partner, discuss the sample answer. Do you think that there are other things that the student could have included in the answer?

4 What mark would you give to this answer out of 6? Look at the mark scheme in the Introduction on page 7 (AO1). What are the reasons for the mark you have given?

Practice questions

1 Look at the photograph below and answer the following questions.

(a) Describe the role of the mu'adhin (muezzin). *(4 marks)*

(b) Explain the part played by the Imam in Friday prayers. *(4 marks)*

(c) 'A woman can never be an Imam.'
What do you think? Explain your opinion. *(3 marks)*

> **Study tip** For a 3-mark evaluation question you must support your opinion with one developed reason or several simple reasons.

(d) Explain the role of the mosque in the Muslim community. *(4 marks)*

> **Study tip** Remember to check the number of marks available for each question. You will need to write a full answer to score 4 marks. Look at the mark scheme in the Introduction and see what kind of answer is likely to gain 4 marks. This is an AO1 question.

(e) 'The money spent on mosques should be spent on helping the poor instead.'
Do you agree? Explain your opinion. *(3 marks)*

(f) 'Mosques are not necessary.'
Do you agree? Give reasons for your answer, showing that you have thought about more than one point of view. *(6 marks)*

4.1 Introduction

■ Lifestyle

Everyone has a **lifestyle**. Some people make deliberate lifestyle choices in the fashion they wear, the food they eat and the activities they take part in. These, and other, lifestyle choices may be limited by opportunity, by wealth or by climate. For example, few people have the chance to live a celebrity lifestyle; no one would need warm clothes in a tropical climate. Many lifestyle choices reflect the character and beliefs of the person making them.

A *Muslims in Mali have a very different lifestyle from Muslims in Britain*

Lifestyle choices

Every Muslim must carry out their duty to God so The Five Pillars are an important part of their lifestyle. The lifestyle choices they have to make are guided by the teaching of Islam. They should not choose to do anything that makes them feel guilty or ashamed, for example, and their lifestyle should not harm them, or anyone else, in any way. For Muslims, the perfect lifestyle is one that obeys the commands of God, makes them happy and contributes in a positive way to society as a whole.

Some lifestyle choices, like the clothes, jewellery and make-up people choose to wear, are about outward show. These, fairly or unfairly, can influence the way people think about you. Muslims want their lives to be an example to others. This is so that other people can learn about Islam from seeing the way that they live. They will think carefully about the choices they make.

Objectives

Explain what is meant by lifestyle and explain some ways in which lifestyle choices are important.

Key terms

Lifestyle: way of life.

Discussion activities

Discuss the following with a partner. Be ready to present your conclusions to the whole class. Read the Study tip before you start.

1 What questions would you ask an Imam about his lifestyle if you were interviewing him for a magazine?

2 If a non-Muslim could follow an Imam around for a day, what do you think they might learn about Islam?

3 How could Muslim teenagers be a good role model for younger Muslims?

⃝⃝ links

To remind yourself about the work of an Imam, see Chapter 3, page 66.

Study tip

When you consider the questions in the Discussion activities, focus on the parts of a Muslim's lifestyle that reflect their faith.

B   *Hands decorated with henna and gold bangles are traditional for a Pakistani Muslim bride*

Is there a Muslim lifestyle?

All Muslim lifestyles express the beliefs and teachings of Islam. However, the way they do this depends on their interpretation of God's law and the country in which they live. When we look at the life of an individual Muslim, it is not always easy to tell which parts of their lifestyle come from Islam. The families of many Muslims in Britain originally came from countries such as Bangladesh, India and Pakistan. Children in these families grow up with their own family traditions. They may have their own fashion, food, manners and, in some cases, language. Non-Muslims, and some younger Muslims, can find it difficult to know which of these customs come from Islam and which are simply the national customs and traditions of the countries from which the families originally came.

D   *Is this type of clothing Islamic or simply a national custom?*

Summary

You should now be able to explain what is meant by lifestyle, and to understand some ways in which lifestyle choices are important.

links

Muslim lifestyle is based on the Qur'an, the hadith and the sunnah. To remind yourself about the hadith and the sunnah, see Chapter 1 page 20.

C   *Typical Asian food, but does Muslim food have to be like this?*

Beliefs and teachings

Much of Muslim lifestyle is based on the sunnah (actions) and hadith (sayings) of the Prophet, like those reported here:

Sunnah of the Prophet
The Prophet used to love to start doing things from the right side whenever possible, for example in performing ritual washing, putting on his shoes, and combing his hair.

Hadith of the Prohet
The Prophet said, that a woman was punished because of a cat which she had imprisoned till it died. She entered the Hell Fire because she did not give it food nor water.

links

See the Muslim lifestyle magazine EMEL for more current issues in Muslim lifestyle:
www.emelmagazine.com.

Beliefs and teachings

Oh believers, eat of the good things we have provided you and give thanks to God.

Qur'an 2:172

Lawful to you is the hunting of water-game (fish) and their use as food.

Qur'an 5:96

Forbidden to you are the meat of animals found dead, blood, and the flesh of swine, and the meat of animals not blessed in the name of God.

Qur'an 5:4

In Islam, food is seen as a gift from God. It is part of God's creation which human beings use for themselves. All Muslims should thank God for what he has given them and Muhammad is said to have ended each meal with the words 'All praise to Him who has given us food and drink and made us Muslims.' Muslims are expected to show their respect for God's gift by not wasting food and by not being greedy or eating more than is good for them.

■ The significance of halal and haram

Two key ideas relating to food are **halal**, meaning lawful, and **haram**, meaning unlawful. The Qur'an forbids a few foods and makes them haram. It forbids Muslims to eat pork, blood, and the meat of any animal not killed in the way commanded by God. Islam also forbids eating most insects. Vegetables and fish are halal, so is most meat, except pork, as long as the animal has been killed in the way commanded by God.

Buying halal food

Halal food shops have to be approved by Muslim authorities so that Muslim shoppers can buy from them with confidence. Where there are no such shops, Muslims have to check the ingredient list for everything they buy, or rely on online lists like the one provided by the Halal Foodguide Service. There are halal butchers in areas of the United Kingdom where there are large numbers of Muslims. Also, major fast-food outlets like Subway have opened halal-only stores in London and Manchester to provide for the Muslim community.

Objectives

Explain and illustrate the ideas of halal and haram.

Key terms

Halal: any action or thing which is permitted or lawful.

Haram: any action or thing which is forbidden.

∞ links

See the website of the Halal Foodguide Service at **www.foodguide.org.uk**.

Activities

1. Explain, using an example, what is meant by halal food.
2. Explain, using an example, what is meant by haram food.

Study tip

Notice that you are being asked to do two things in Activities 1 and 2. Make sure you do both.

A *When this symbol is seen on restaurants or foods, Muslims know that all the ingredients are halal*

B *Ordinary British food can be halal*

C *An Indian dish. This may be halal*

Recognising halal food

Many Muslims in this country are from India, Pakistan and Bangladesh. They have their own traditional food but halal food does not have to be like that. Fish and chips can be halal but the ingredients, and how it was cooked, would have to be checked to make sure that it was. One big problem would be the fat that the fish and chips had been cooked in. It could be animal fat from haram animals, and haram foods may also have been cooked in it. It is not always obvious which foods contain haram ingredients. Gelatine is often used to set fillings and jellies but it is made from the boiled bones and skin of animals including pigs. This means that anything with gelatine in it is haram. There are vegetarian alternatives. If they are used, the food may be halal.

Research activity 🔍

Using the internet, find out how much halal food is available in the major supermarkets.

D *Haram ingredients like gelatine may be hidden in food like this*

Extension activity

Write a letter to a sweet manufacturer, asking them to find a replacement for gelatine in their sweets. You will need to explain why Muslims cannot eat anything that contains gelatine.

Summary

You should now be able to explain and illustrate the ideas of halal and haram, in relation to food in particular.

Beliefs and teachings

They ask you what is lawful to them (as food). Say: lawful unto you are (all) things good and pure: and what you have taught your trained hunting animals (to catch) in the manner directed to you by Allah. Eat what they catch for you, but pronounce the name of Allah over it.

Qur'an 5:5

Food preparation

All animals that are provided by God for food have to be treated properly when they are alive and killed painlessly when the time comes. Meat is only halal, meaning lawful, if the animal was blessed in the name of God before it was killed and then it was killed by a single cut to the throat. Muhammad told his followers that they should sharpen their knives so that the animal did not suffer. Areas where food is prepared should be clean and free from any unlawful ingredients. Some Muslims prefer to have their food prepared by other Muslims so that they can be sure that it is halal.

Objectives

Explore how food is prepared in Islam and the significance of food laws for Muslims today.

Research activity

Some people object to the Islamic method of slaughter, although Muslims are sure that, when it is done properly, it is painless. Find out how animals are usually slaughtered in the UK and why some people think this is a better method.

A   *Muslims can buy with confidence from a halal butcher*

Case study

David's party

When Adeel went to David's party last year it had been a disaster. He had enjoyed playing with the other children, but when it was time to eat he was not so happy. In front of him were meat sandwiches, crisps, sausages and cheese as well as some lovely looking cakes. David's mother had seen that he wasn't eating and had been worried that he was ill. He had explained that he could not eat any of the food because he did not know if it was halal. This year everything was great. David's mum had checked all the ingredients and there was lots of halal food which everyone enjoyed.

B   *These cakes look inviting, but they may be haram*

These rules are not always easy to keep in the United Kingdom. This is because most animals are not killed in the way laid down by Islamic law. Also many different types of food contain animal ingredients. Some biscuits, cakes and sweets include the red food dye cochineal, which is made from a type of beetle. This means that they are haram, as well as the more obvious things like pork sausages and bacon. Muslims are expected to make every effort to keep these rules. However, the Qur'an makes it clear that if a Muslim eats a forbidden ingredient without knowing it, or is forced by hunger to eat a forbidden food, this is not a sin.

C   *These sweets look good – but are they halal?*

■ The importance of the food laws

These dietary rules protect the animals that are to be eaten. They also play a special part in Muslim life. They unite the Muslim community and keep them apart from non-Muslims. They unite them because they encourage them to live in areas where there are already other Muslims and halal shops. They also encourage them to eat only with other Muslims. They keep them apart from non-Muslims by making it difficult for Muslims to share the food of non-Muslims. Many Muslim leaders feel this is a good thing, especially for young people who might be misled into non-Islamic ways by non-Muslim friends. However, many non-Muslims will try to make sure that they provide food for their friends which is halal and will ask if they are not sure.

Activity

'Eating a special diet is nothing to do with religion.' What do you think? Explain your opinion.

Summary

You should now understand how food is prepared in Islam, and be aware of the significance of food laws for Muslims today. Keeping these laws unites the Muslim community and separates them from non-Muslims.

Discussion activity

Some people object to eating meat under any circumstances. If we could be sure that the animal did not suffer, would that make it acceptable to eat meat?

Extension activity

Imagine that you are a Muslim using non-Muslim caterers for a wedding. What special instructions will you have to give them to make sure that the food is halal? Think about the meat that will be used, other ingredients and how the food will be prepared.

D   *The Chinese cook is preparing halal food*

Study tip

The key to good answers is often good examples. Find examples of popular foods that are or may be haram and make sure that you can explain why they are haram.

4.4 Alcohol

Intoxicants and gambling, idol worship and games of chance, are works of the devil; Avoid them, so that you may succeed. The devil wants to cause anger and hatred among you through intoxicants and gambling, and to distract you from remembering God, and from observing the Prayers.

Qur'an 5:90

Objectives

Consider Muslim attitudes to alcohol and their importance.

Muslims take this verse from the Qur'an to mean that God has forbidden alcohol and anything else, like drugs, that can confuse the mind and leave people with little or no control over their actions. They believe that God has given this command, like all his others, for the benefit of human beings. Being a Muslim means always being in control of what you think, say and do. Alcohol abuse prevents this. Drunks can be a danger to themselves and others but Islam forbids self-harm and harm to others. This, according to Muslim teachers, is why God has forbidden alcohol. There is clear evidence that people do damage their health though drinking alcohol. There is also evidence that drinking alcohol leads many people to do things that they regret afterwards. These can include violence, drink-driving, sex before marriage and many other things which clearly break Islamic law. Drinking alcohol can also lead to loss of self-esteem and arguments. Not drinking alcohol helps people avoid these sins.

A *Islam teaches that God has forbidden alcohol for our own good*

Muslims in the UK do not always find it easy to avoid alcohol. This is partly because so many people do drink alcohol that it is simply part of the way of life and it is easy to find in supermarkets and shops. Also, it is apparently something that gives a lot of pleasure to many people. Every celebration seems to involve alcohol. Birthdays, weddings, passing exams, family gatherings or simply spending time with friends; all of these occasions may be celebrated by opening bottles of wine, spirits or beer. Another reason is that not all foodstuffs are labelled clearly. In February 2008, for example, it was discovered that a well-known brand of crisps contained small amounts of alcohol, although the packaging did not mention it.

Some Muslims believe that God has forbidden Muslims from handling alcohol in any form, for example, in shops and at supermarket checkouts.

B 'Allah has cursed wine, its drinker, its server, its buyer' (Hadith)

C Could a Muslim do this job?

Others believe that God has only forbidden drinking alcohol because of the dangers of drunkenness. They believe that it can be used for any good purpose, for example, in antiseptic hand-washes used to prevent the spread of infections. Some Muslims feel that it is acceptable to drink alcohol as long as you do not get drunk. However, a generally accepted hadith of the Prophet forbids having even a small amount of anything that intoxicates. However, Islamic teaching makes it clear that eating or drinking alcohol by mistake, which is when you did not know you were doing it, is not a sin.

Discussion activity

Should a Muslim work or eat in a restaurant that serves alcohol?

Study tip

Your sentences should be short and clear.

Research activity

Find out what the Qur'an has to say about using alcohol : Qur'an 4:43; 2:219 and 5:90–91.

Summary

You should now be able to discuss Muslim attitudes to alcohol, and to understand the importance of what Islam teaches about the dangers of alcohol abuse.

Activity

1 Sum up the Muslim attitude to alcohol in three sentences that answer these questions:

a Sentence 1: What does God command?

b Sentence 2: Why does God command this?

c Sentence 3: What uses of alcohol does Islam allow?

Beliefs and teachings

We have given you clothing to cover your shame and as a decoration for you. The clothing of righteousness, that is the best.

Qur'an 7:26

According to this verse from the Qur'an, God has commanded human beings to wear clothes for two reasons: to cover the body and to make the person look better. There are many different styles of Islamic dress which show different interpretations of the guidelines found in the Qur'an, especially when it comes to women's dress.

Both men and women are expected to show **modesty** in the clothes they wear. Women are expected to dress in a way that shows that they are Muslims. The Qur'an instructs the Prophet to 'tell your wives and daughters, and the believing women, to wrap their clothes around themselves so that they are recognised and not hurt' (Qur'an 33:59). Women are also told not to display their finery. This means that dress is meant to protect the wearer and to prevent Muslims from taking too much pride in their appearance. It is also a way Muslims can develop the type of relationships between men and women that Islam requires.

A *Some women stay in purdah when they leave the house by choosing clothing which leaves no part of the body showing except the eyes*

Purdah

This is the practice of preventing women from being seen by men, except their closest male relatives. Some Muslims believe that **purdah** is a cultural rather than a religious practice. That means that it is a custom or tradition developed in some Muslim societies rather than part of the teaching of Islam. Keeping purdah means separating men and women as far as possible, for example, by giving them separate entrances to the mosque and separate prayer rooms, and separate social events. The practice also requires arranged marriages and means that when a woman appears in public she must follow a very strict dress code.

Objectives

Explain and illustrate what is meant by purdah and hijab and the importance of these for Muslims.

Key terms

Modesty: unpretentious manner or appearance.

Purdah: an Urdu word often used to describe complete seclusion. Women covering their face and hands when in public.

Hijab: modest dress for women – often used to mean the veil or headscarf Muslim women wear – means 'cover'.

Activity

1　What do you think non-Muslims in Britain today would think of as 'modest dress'?

B *In this style of dress from Afghanistan, even the eyes cannot be seen*

The traditional rules for modest dress drawn up by the scholars

For women:

- Clothing must cover the entire body, except the face and hands.
- Clothing should be loose so that the shape of the body is not seen.

For men:

- Clothing must cover the body from navel to knee.
- Clothing should be loose so that the shape of the body is not seen.

C   *Omani Muslim men in traditional dress*

■ Hijab

The word **hijab** is often used for the headscarf or veil commonly worn by women in Muslim countries. The use of the hijab is based on the Qur'an and on the hadith of the Prophet. In one hadith he says, "When the woman reaches puberty, no part of her body should be seen but this, and he pointed to his face and his hands." As a result, women often cover their hair with a hijab. More generally, hijab can also mean modest dress.

D   *The hijab is commonly worn by Muslim women*

Activity

2   Why should Muslim women wear modest dress? Find and write down **four** reasons mentioned in this section.

Summary

You should now know that purdah is the tradition that a woman should not be seen by men, except those most closely related to her, and that the hijab is the headscarf or veil worn by Muslim women. Both are designed to help ensure modesty.

Study tip

When you are asked a straightforward question, always answer the question directly. The answer to 'Why should Muslim women wear modest dress?' should begin with: 'Muslim women should wear modest dress because…' This helps to make sure you keep to the point.

Various styles of hijab are worn all over the world but some Muslim women do not wear it at all. Many outsiders think that women are forced to wear the hijab by men. This is clearly not how some of the women see it. They are proud to wear the hijab as an outward sign of their faith. At the 2008 Olympics, female Muslim athletes from several countries, including Egypt, Afghanistan and Iran, competed wearing the hijab.

Research activities

1. Using the internet, find out about the latest Muslim fashions. You may find the following websites helpful: www.2hijab.com www.trendyhijab.com

2. Find out more about the veiled athletes at the 2008 Olympic Games using the internet.

A   *Veiled athletes from Pakistan*

Another reason women give for wearing the hijab is that it makes men treat them as people. They feel that women in countries like Britain are only valued by men for their looks, and that western women have to dress to please men if they are going to get on in society. However, Muslim women want to be treated as individuals, not as beautiful objects on display for men to see.

B   *The hijab can be a fashion statement*

Case study

The value of a woman

In Britain, women and girls are valued for their looks. Men want to be seen with a beautiful woman just to impress their friends. It is as if having a pretty woman at their side is proof that they are successful and important; Women who like that kind of attention do not value themselves; they are only worried about their appearance, and whether men fancy them or not. Muslim women do value themselves. We want to be respected for our character and intelligence, so we wear the hijab. Our appearance is private and precious, we don't want to share it with everyone. We want to be able to give the gift of seeing it only to our husbands. We want to be respected. We want people to know that we are respectable when they see us. Men value each other for their friendship, kindness and company. We want them to value us in the same way.

Aisha, a 17-year-old Muslim girl from Birmingham

In contrast, some Muslims do not think that it is necessary for women to wear the hijab. Based on the second part of Qur'an 7:26 'the clothing of righteousness is best', they argue that hijab is not just about the clothes people wear but is a way of behaving and an attitude. Special clothing may be a way of helping women, and men, to achieve this but it is not necessary. To keep hijab from this point of view is to keep to the laws of Islam for male/female relationships, to avoid having too much pride in your appearance and to dress in a way that does not deliberately draw attention to yourself. How the woman does this is her choice.

C   *Some Muslim girls wear the hijab all the time in public*

Summary

You should now be aware of at least two different attitudes to the hijab. One view is that wearing the hijab shows that a woman is respectable. An alternative view is that the hijab is an attitude and a way of behaving.

Activity

1   Read the Case study.

a   Give three reasons why Aisha has chosen to wear the hijab.

b   The way she appears is very important to a Muslim woman. Do you agree? Give reasons for your answer showing that you have thought about more than one point of view.

Study tip

You should be able to express your views about the hijab and to be able to argue both for and against the view that Muslim women should wear the hijab.

Activities

2   'People should not judge you how by how you dress.' Do you agree?

3   Does wearing the hijab make you a good Muslim?

4   Would not wearing the hijab make you a poor Muslim?

5   Can you think of any situations in which Muslims should not wear the hijab?

Beliefs and teachings

You are the best community given to human beings. You command what is right and forbid what is indecent, and you believe in Allah.

Qur'an 3:110

The **Ummah** is the Muslim community of believers. Anyone can join the Ummah because its members are linked by faith and by their commitment to the shahadah. As soon as someone says the words 'There is no god but God, and Muhammad is the Prophet of God' in front of witnesses from the community, they have become a member of the Ummah. From that moment on, the whole community will support the new Muslim as he or she tries to follow the laws, customs and traditions of Islam.

When someone becomes a Muslim and a member of the Ummah, they take on a Muslim name. This shows their new identity and their new understanding of their relationship with God. Many male names start with Abdul, meaning servant, followed by one of the names of God. For example, Abdul Ghaffar, servant of the Forgiver, and Abdul Basseer, servant of the All-Seeing. Female names include Aamilah, meaning 'she who does good works', and Samina, meaning 'precious and generous'.

All Muslims see themselves as brothers or sisters of all other Muslims. A Muslim's relationship with God and with other Muslims is seen as more important than their relationship with their birth family. This is what the Prophet taught his followers when they emigrated to Madinah and left their non-believing birth families behind.

> 66 *Muslims by virtue of their faith in Allah and His Prophet, are one Ummah and are brothers to each other – a relationship which stands above that of blood. If a blood relationship stands in the way of Islam, it is to be rejected in favour of faith.* 99
>
> *Muhammad Manazir Ahsan*

The modern Ummah includes people from all nations and races. They all have the same rights and responsibilities. Everyone is equal regardless of their skin colour, language and gender because all that matters is how good a Muslim they are. This worldwide Ummah is linked by a shared language, the Arabic of the Qur'an and of the prayers. All Muslims practise The Five Pillars, follow the Shari'ah, the holy law of Islam, and have customs based on the sunnah of the Prophet. Most Muslims still live in the Middle East, but there are Muslims all over the world.

In a non-Muslim country like Britain, the Muslim Ummah is one of many communities that make up society as a whole. It not only has its own beliefs, values, customs and traditions but also its own pace of life built around the yearly cycle of its calendar and the daily routine of prayers. It has its own food and dress code and, in some places, its own schools. All these things unite the community and make it stand apart from the rest.

Objectives

Explain what the Ummah is and what links the community together.

Key terms

Ummah: all Muslims are regarded as part of a brotherhood; the nation of Islam.

∞ **links**

For more details about the shahadah, see Chapter 2, pages 38–39.

Research activity 🔍

For more information about Muslim names and their meaning, see www.muslim-names.co.uk or a similar website.

A *Amir Khan: member of the Ummah and British boxer*

B   *Baroness Warsi: Sayeeda Warsi is a member of the Ummah and the House of Lords*

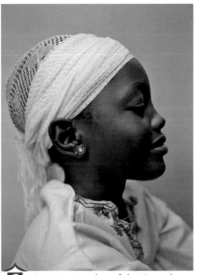

C   *A young member of the Ummah from Africa*

D   *An older Arab member of the Ummah*

E   *Estimated Muslim populations 2008*

Country	Number of Muslims
Indonesia	204 million
Pakistan	164 million
India	154 million
Bangladesh	128 million
Turkey	76 million
Egypt	74 million
Nigeria	73 million
Iran	65 million
Morocco	34 million
Algeria	33 million
Afghanistan	32 million
Saudi Arabia	28 million
Sudan	28 million
China	27 million
Iraq	27 million
Ethiopia	27 million

F   *An estimated two million Muslims live in the UK*

Study tip

Read each question carefully. Many candidates lose marks because they misread the question that has been set.

Summary

You should now understand what the Ummah is and what links the community together. The Muslim Ummah is the worldwide community of believers; they are linked by faith, not by birth, and are expected to support each other.

Activities

1   Who can become a member of the Muslim Ummah?
2   How does someone become a member of the Muslim Ummah?
3   Who are a Muslim's brothers and sisters?
4   Why do many Muslim names begin with 'Abdul'?
5   Give two things that all members of the Ummah have in common.

4.8 Respect, religious duties and good actions

You who believe, do not let one set of people make fun of another; do not insult one another by calling each other names; do not spy on one another, or spread rumours about each other or criticise people behind their backs.

Summary of Qur'an 49:10–12

Objectives

Explain how the Muslim community shows respect for each other and carries out its religious duties and good actions.

Respect

Every Muslim has rights given to them by God. Every other Muslim has a duty to respect and protect those rights. Muhammad said that the life, property and honour of one Muslim are sacred to another. He also said that a true believer is one who wants for his brother what he wants for himself.

Case study

How to show respect

Respect the property of others. If something belongs to another person, do not steal it, or damage it. If you are lent it take good care of it and return it as soon as you have finished with it.

Respect the feelings of others. Do not bully or tease; do not frighten them, or upset them, without reason. If you have bad news to tell them, tell them gently.

Respect their privacy. Do not enter their homes without an invitation; do not demand their news but allow them to offer it instead.

Treat everyone you meet with good manners to show that you recognise that they are as important as you.

Respect yourself. You are valued by God and have a duty to care for yourself. Keep yourself fit.

A *The elderly should be treated with respect*

1. Read the case study. Choose one type of respect (e.g. respect for privacy or respect for self) and write a list to tell someone what they should do and what they should not do to show this type of respect. Put what you should do under the heading 'Do' and what you should not do under the heading 'Do not'.

2. Do you think people generally treat each other with respect? Give an example where respect was shown and another where it was not.

Religious duties

The religious duties of the Ummah are to carry out The Five Pillars, to celebrate the festivals, to obey the laws of God and to follow the example of the Prophet. Some of these duties like prayer and fasting, they can do together. Others, like hajj, only a few will be able to do. However, the rest can learn from their experience. In order for the local Ummah to carry out these duties, some Muslims have to take on special roles. The community needs experts in the Qur'an and Shari'ah law to make sure that the true teachings are not forgotten. It needs judges to settle disputes between Muslims and rule on matters like divorce. It needs representatives who will speak for the community as a whole, both to the government and to other Muslims worldwide. The community must provide and support the people in these special roles so that everyone can live life as God intended it to be lived.

⦾links

For more information on the Shari'ah, see Chapter 1, pages 30–31.

■ Good actions and Sadaqah

Good actions are expected from all Muslims. The feeling of brotherhood and sisterhood between Muslims should be so strong that if any Muslim hears that another is in need, they should immediately ask, 'What can I do to help?' As one hadith of the Prophet says, 'You cannot enter paradise unless you are a total believer. You cannot be a total believer unless you love one another.' This means that every Muslim must be generous with their time and their money to help those around them. This is the duty of Sadaqah or charity. For Muhammad, charity was far more than giving money. Sadaqah includes everything from praising God to helping people in any way possible. Even smiling at people is considered Sadaqah. Some people think that doing good actions like this is more important than praying or fasting.

The Prophet commanded Muslims to care for their neighbours, both Muslim and non-Muslim.

> ❝ *Show him concern if he is distressed*
> *Nurse him when he is ill*
> *Attend his funeral if he dies*
> *Congratulate him if he meets any good*
> *Sympathise with him if any calamity befall him*
> *Do not block his air by raising your building high without his permission*
> *Harass him not*
> *Give him a share when you buy fruits, and, if you do not, bring what you buy quietly and let not your children take them out to excite the jealousy of his children.* ❞
> *Adapted from Islam the Natural Way, A W Hamid (1992)*

⚭ links

See the Glossary for a definition of the term 'Sadaqah'.

Activity

3 Think about the place of prayer and Sadaqah in the life of a Muslim. 'I can't help on Friday lunchtime because I haven't got enough time to help. I need to go to the prayer.' What do you think an Imam would say about this?

Extension activity

Write a leaflet for a Muslim child with the title: 'How to be a good member of the Ummah.'

Activity

4 Suggest some practical ways in which Muslims may be able to help others.

Study tip

Good examples can help you to explain how Muslims are expected to help others.

B *The work of the Red Crescent aid organisation is one way in which the Ummah carries out good works*

C *The dead should be respected as well as the living*

Summary

You should now be able to explain how the Muslim community shows respect for each other and carries out its religious duties and good actions.

4.9 The importance of lifestyle and community

The importance of the Muslim lifestyle

In Islam, it is not enough just to believe. Those beliefs expressed in the shahadah must lead to action. If you do not live a Muslim lifestyle, you are not a Muslim. Islam is not just a set of beliefs and a pattern of ritual worship, it is a complete way of life to be followed 'from cradle to grave', that is, from birth to death. The first great belief of the shahadah is that there is only one God. This means that a Muslim's lifestyle must show that there is nothing in life that is more important than God, and that service to God must always come first. This is what the pillars train Muslims to do. Muslims must make sure that service to God is more important than, among other things, making money, following family tradition, or following fashion. Anyone who fails to do this is not a Muslim. This is because they have allowed their life to be ruled by someone or something more important to them than God.

The second part of the shahadah is the belief that Muhammad is God's messenger. What this means for the Muslim lifestyle is that Muhammad set the standard that other Muslims must try to live up to. What he did, as a father and husband for example, and what he said, for example, about the role of women, is the model for others to follow. There are different opinions about how much of Muhammad's example is relevant today and how accurately his example is recorded. However, Muslims agree that in any situation they should do what Muhammad would have done.

Objectives

Consider the importance both of the Muslim lifestyle and of living as part of a community.

Extension activity

'Love of money or love of God?' In what ways might someone show that money is more important to them than God?

Study tip

In the Extension activity, think of actions that could bring you money but which are against the law of God.

A *Friendship plays an important part the Islamic community*

B *The shahadah. It is not enough to believe these words; they must also be put into action*

Beliefs and teachings

God does not look at your bodies and appearance, he looks at your hearts and your deeds.

Hadith

The Muslim lifestyle is not just about doing the right thing. Muhammad taught that the value of an action depended on the intention behind it. This means that anyone who chooses to dress or behave in a Muslim way just to impress those around them is not serving God and is not living a Muslim life.

The importance of the community

> ### Beliefs and teachings
>
> Believers should be like the bricks of a building. Every brick is supported and strengthened by another.
>
> *Hadith*

Islam teaches that it is very important for every Muslim to play a full part in the life of the community. Meeting other Muslims gives believers a chance to get to know each other and to build friendships. This means that every Muslim should have someone to call on if they need help or advice. Muhammad taught that someone was only really poor if they dared not ask another person for help. This means that it is the duty of every Muslim to support each other.

Muslims believe that we need other people to make us really happy. Other people can encourage and motivate us. They can help us not to be worried or frightened when we try something new. Whatever we are doing, other people have done before us and we can learn from their successes and failures. Where there are only a few Muslims in the area, having each other for support can be really important.

The online generation

Some Muslim leaders are worried about those young people who prefer to do everything online rather than face-to-face. It is possible to declare the shahadah online and, by using chat rooms and educational websites, Muslims can talk to each other and learn about Islam without ever meeting a real Muslim. The people they meet online may be the other side of the world and of no help at all when real-life problems come up.

C *Study is an important duty for Muslims*

D *The Ummah must teach its children and bring them up as Muslims*

Discussion activity

Are these online services a good thing? Think about Muslims in different situations as you answer this question: for example, the only Muslim working on an oil rig in the North Sea; a shy young man who finds it difficult to make friends; a young widow living in a different part of the country from her family and friends; a badly disabled Muslim who cannot leave the house.

Summary

You should now understand the importance both of the Muslim lifestyle and of living as part of a community. You cannot be a Muslim without living a Muslim lifestyle, and to be really happy Muslims need the company and support of the community.

Activities

1. Name two things that some people might make more important than service to God.

2. Give two ways in which members of a community can support each other.

3. Give one way in which the internet can help someone to be a good Muslim.

4. Give one way in which the internet could stop someone from being a happy Muslim.

4

Personal lifestyle – summary

For the examination, you should be able to:

✔ explain what is meant by lifestyle and why lifestyle choices are important

✔ explain and illustrate the ideas of halal and haram

✔ understand Muslim attitudes to diet and food preparation

✔ consider Muslim attitudes to the prohibition of alcohol

✔ know and understand Muslim attitudes to dress, purdah, the concept of modesty and the hijab

✔ understand Muslim attitudes to shahadah

✔ explain the meaning of Ummah and consider what links the members of the community together

✔ explain how Muslims show respect to each other and carry out religious duties and good actions.

Sample answer

1 Write an answer to the following examination question:

Explain Muslim teaching about diet.   (*6 marks*)

2 Read the following sample answer:

> Muslims are expected to follow God's law in what they eat. Their food must be halal. That means it must not have any haram ingredients. Any meat they eat must come from an animal that has been killed in the way given by God in the Qur'an. They must also eat healthy food.

3 With a partner, discuss the sample answer. How could the answer be improved?

4 What mark would you give this answer out of 6? Look at the mark scheme in the Introduction on page 7 (AO1). What are the reasons for the mark you have given?

Practice questions

1 Look at the photograph below and answer the following questions.

(a) Explain what Muslims understand by 'modest dress'. *(4 marks)*

(b) Explain why many Muslims do not drink alcohol. *(4 marks)*

(c) 'Wearing special clothes does not make you a good person.'
Do you agree? Give reasons for your answer, showing that
you have thought about more than one point of view.
Refer to Islam in your answer. *(6 marks)*

(d) Explain what Muslims understand by the Ummah. *(4 marks)*

(e) 'A good Muslim must play a full part in the life of the community.'
Do you agree? Give reasons for your answer, showing that you
have thought about more than one point of view. *(6 marks)*

5.1 The marriage ceremony

Marriage is strongly recommended in Islam and most Muslims believe that it is their duty to marry and have children as Muhammad did. Marriage is celebrated in different ways in different parts of the Muslim world. However, there are three key features: the willing consent of both partners, the marriage contract and the dowry.

Willing consent

Both parties must willingly agree to the marriage in front of at least two trustworthy witnesses. This is to make sure that no one is forced to marry, because this is forbidden in Islam. The Prophet cancelled one woman's marriage when she complained that she had been forced into it. Each person is simply asked if they will accept the other as their husband or wife. When they answer 'Yes' two copies of the contract are signed and exchanged and the marriage is sealed.

The contract

A marriage contract is drawn up by the couple or their families. It sets out what each partner can expect from the other. It often includes an agreement about what will happen if the marriage fails and ends in divorce. The idea of a contract is fairly new, and quite fashionable, in British society where it is called a pre-nuptial agreement. It has existed in Islam for over 1000 years.

A A bride signs the wedding contract

Objectives

Recall the main parts of the marriage ceremony and consider the importance of the ceremony.

Key terms

Marriage: a legal union between a man and a woman.

Extension activity

Explain why willing consent is such an important part of the marriage ceremony.

Beliefs and teachings

Marriage is part of my sunnah.

Hadith

Part of a marriage contract

A wife must:

- Bring up her children as Muslims
- Run the home efficiently
- Obey her husband unless he orders her to break God's law
- Dress modestly outside the home
- Be faithful and not have sex outside the marriage relationship

B A British Muslim wedding

Part of a marriage contract

A husband must:

- Always act towards his wife according to the teachings of Islam
- Support his family and provide them with food and clothing
- Be faithful and not have sex outside the marriage relationship

The dowry

The husband is commanded by the Qur'an to give a wedding gift of money or possessions to his wife. She may do with it whatever she chooses. In Shi'ah Islam this must be paid as the contract is signed. In Sunni Islam it may be paid in stages.

In some Muslim societies, where purdah is traditionally practised, two separate ceremonies will take place: one for the bride, the other for the groom. These may happen in different rooms or even different buildings. The witnesses, who normally include the father of the bride and the groom, will hear the bride willingly agree to the marriage and will then represent her at the groom's ceremony. The new wife is then brought to her husband so that married life can begin.

The significance of the marriage ceremony

Marriage is a contract between the couple and it unites the two families. It is the duty of the Muslim Ummah to make sure that the terms of the marriage contract are kept to. This is why the contract is read out for all to hear and a copy of it is kept in the mosque. In British law this contract is not legally binding. There will have to be a civil ceremony as well if the husband and wife want the rights that British law gives to married couples.

Muslims are encouraged to treat the marriage as a lifelong commitment, but the contract only lasts as long as both partners keep to it. Islam allows divorce if the marriage breaks down.

Activity

2 These questions will help you test your understanding of what you have read.

a Explain the meaning of each of the following: (i) marriage contract (ii) dowry.

b Why is it important that there are witnesses to the marriage ceremony?

c Give an example of **one** promise a man may make as part of the marriage contract.

d Give an example of **one** promise a woman may make as part of the marriage contract.

e 'Muslims can divorce when they want to. This means that they do not need to take marriage seriously.' Do you agree? Give reasons for your answer.

Activity

1 Read the marriage contract.

a Are there any other conditions that you would want to include in the contract?

b Compare the agreement made by the man with the agreement made by the woman. Do the differences between them support the idea that marriage is an equal partnership?

Research activity 🔍

Find out more about marriage ceremonies in Islam. See www.bbc.co.uk/religion and follow the links to 'Islam' and 'Rites and rituals'.

Study tip

Make sure that you can look at marriage from the point of view of both the man and the woman.

Summary

You should now be able to recall the main parts of a Muslim marriage ceremony, and to consider the importance of the ceremony. The essential parts of a Muslim marriage ceremony are willing consent from both partners, a marriage contract and a dowry.

Case study

Nabeenah's wedding diary

The day before

The celebrations started the day before the wedding. My cousins, aunts and other female friends of the family came to my house. We sang and danced and there were lovely things to eat. Then Fatima put the henna designs on my hands and my feet. It took a long time, and I had to sit very still. When she had finished everyone agreed that they looked wonderful.

My wedding day

The groom's party arrived early. I could hear them long before I could see them. Their music was so loud, I think everyone around must have heard them coming. I was already wearing my beautiful red robes, and bangles which looked lovely on my decorated hands. I watched his family arrive from the upstairs landing. He didn't see me, but he told me later that he knew that I was watching.

When the time came I joined all the ladies in the upstairs room. My father arrived with Arshan's father and three other people. The Maulvi, a local religious teacher, was conducting the ritual. He told me that Arshan wanted to marry me and asked me if I was willing. I said 'Yes' immediately, but he asked me two times more just to make sure. Then the contract was read out; my friends were impressed by the dowry he was paying me. Arshad had already signed it, so I signed it, so did my dad and his dad, and the Maulvi.

Then I was taken to the room where Arshad and his family were waiting. It was so exciting. He gave me the dowry envelope and then we were given two thrones to sit on. They treated us like a king and queen. The Maulvi recited some verses from the Qur'an and reminded us that it was important to remember God at all times. Then the celebrations really began with food, song and dancing. Neighbours arrived from all around. Everyone was invited. I was so happy.

A *A red robed bride with decorated hands*

B *The Maulvi holds the marriage contract as the groom signs it*

C *Many people choose to marry in a register office*

Maryam's wedding

Case study

Maryam's wedding took place in a British register office. Her parents were still in India so they could not attend, but her brother and his wife were there, and some friends to act as witnesses. The registrar made sure that they understood the meaning of what they were doing and asked them both if they agreed to marry each other. When they said they did, the register was signed by Maryam, her husband, the witnesses and the registrar. Afterwards they all went for a meal, and that evening Maryam and her new husband celebrated with all their friends.

Activity

1   Read the accounts of the weddings of Nabeenah and Maryam.

a   What are the main differences between the two weddings?

b   What are the main similarities between the weddings?

c   Why might some Muslims prefer the first type of wedding?

d   Why might some Muslims prefer the second type of wedding?

e   'A religious person should always have a religious wedding.' What do you think? Explain your opinion.

D   *A wedding feast*

Afrah's wedding

Case study

Afrah was only sixteen. She didn't really understand the words her uncle told her to say because they weren't in English, but she did what she was told. Afterwards her aunt told her that she was now married and would be leaving their home to live with her husband and his family.

Beliefs and teachings

The worst of feasts are those marriage feasts to which the rich are invited and the poor are left out.

Hadith

He who refuses to accept an invitation to a marriage feast disobeys God and his Prophet.

Hadith

Activity

2   Read the account of Afrah's wedding. Most Muslims would not accept this as a valid Muslim wedding – why not?

E   *Jordanian brides in a mass Muslim wedding*

Summary

You should now be aware of many different styles of Muslim wedding and realise that the type of wedding people decide to have may depend on the family situation.

Study tip

You may use examples as evidence to support your point of view.

5.3 Divorce and remarriage

Islam does not forbid **divorce** but it strongly disapproves of it.

Beliefs and teachings

The Qur'an on divorce

A divorce must be pronounced twice: after that, the parties should either stay together on honourable terms, or separate with kindness. It is not lawful for you, to take back any of your gifts from your wives, except when both parties fear that they would be unable to keep the limits ordained by Allah.

Qur'an 2.229

If you fear a divorce between them, appoint two judges one from his family, one from hers. If they wish for peace, Allah will cause their reconciliation.

Qur'an 4:35

Divorced women shall wait for three monthly periods. Nor is it lawful for them to hide what Allah Hath created in their wombs, if they have faith in Allah and the Last Day.

Qur'an 2:228

If a husband divorces his wife he cannot remarry her until she has married another husband and he has divorced her.

Qur'an 2:230

A *A happy Muslim couple*

How men can divorce their wives

Men can divorce their wives simply by saying these words to her three times: 'I divorce you.' This practice is based on the Qur'an, but there are different interpretations of how this should be done.

- When the man first tells his wife that he is divorcing her, there should be a three month period during which the couple and their families do everything they can to bring about a reconciliation. Only if that fails may the man repeat the words twice more and make the divorce final.

- The man can simply say the statement three times to his wife on the same occasion. Some scholars accept this as a valid divorce; others argue that it counts only as one statement of divorce and that there must be a period of reconciliation before the divorce is final.

How a wife divorces her husband

The couple may have agreed in the marriage contract that the woman has the same right to divorce her husband as he has to divorce her. In most cases the woman has to apply to a local Shari'ah court for a divorce. In Britain this often means applying to the Islamic Shari'ah Council which is based in London. The purpose of the court is to give rulings on any aspect of Shari'ah law. It consists of judges who are experts on the law.

On her application form, the woman will have to explain why she wants a divorce. There are many reasons why she may be given one, including the husband's adultery, violence, desertion or breaking of the marriage contract. The Council will want to discuss the wife's application with the husband and to make sure that there has been a serious attempt at reconciliation. The Council will also decide what should happen to the dowry. If the divorce is not the woman's fault, she usually keeps it.

Remarriage

A man may remarry as soon as the divorce is finalised. A woman has to wait for at least three months. The Qur'an (2:228) suggests that this is because she could be pregnant. This is because if she were, her ex-husband would be financially responsible for the child. When the Qur'an was revealed, 1400 years ago, this law made complete sense. Today some Muslims think it is not necessary. The divorced couple cannot marry each other again, unless the woman has married and divorced someone else in the meantime. **Remarriage** is strongly advised in Islam because men and women are not believed to be complete or truly happy unless they are married.

B The Shari'ah Council considers an application for a divorce

Research activity

Find out how the Shari'ah Council investigates an application for divorce. You may find the following website useful: www.islamic-sharia.org

Study tip

When you are discussing this issue, think about the different responsibilities men and women have after a divorce.

Key terms

Remarriage: when people who have been married before marry again.

Discussion activity

4 Can you see any other advantages for woman waiting at least three months after a divorce before she remarries?

Children and divorce

It is the father's responsibility to provide for his children, so divorced fathers are expected to pay towards their children's upbringing. It is generally agreed that young children should stay with their mother, but there are different opinions about what should happen when they are older. Some think that children older than seven should be with their father. Other arrangements may have been part of the marriage contract.

Extension activity

'A good Muslim couple should never divorce.' What do you think? Explain your opinion.

Discussion activity

5 Men do not have to explain why they want a divorce, but women do.

a Is this fair?

b What do you think? Explain your opinion.

Summary

You should now know the procedures for divorce and remarriage in Islam, and understand their significance. Divorce is permitted in Islam. Men can divorce their wives; women must apply for a divorce.

5.4 Arranged marriages

In traditional Muslim societies, men and women do not mix freely. When the time comes for them to marry, their parents will find and introduce them to a suitable partner. This is known as an **arranged marriage**. The two families may have known each other a long time and they may be related. In some cases, the son and daughter will have grown up knowing that their parents planned for them to marry. But arranged marriages are not forced marriages. The young people do not have to marry the person their parents have introduced them to. Arranged marriages are sometimes called introduction marriages or assisted marriages, because the parents only help their children find the right partner. They do not make the decision for them.

A An arranged marriage can mean that the husband does not see his wife's face until after the ceremony

Other ways of finding a partner

Most people in Britain do not have an arranged marriage. They try to find a suitable partner for themselves. Many are successful and have long and happy marriages, but others get it wrong. Almost half the marriages that take place in Britain each year end in divorce. Young people look for partners at school, university or work. They meet people in clubs, pubs and discos. They use chat rooms or online dating agencies. Some of these methods are dangerous; some are simply not real options for believing Muslims.

Arranged marriage or love match

A so-called love match is when a couple meet each other, fall in love, and decide to marry as a result. In an arranged marriage, love between the two may come after the wedding rather than before it. In other words, if the couple are well-matched in terms of interests, background and education, love may grow as the marriage progresses. Some people have very clear views about both love matches and arranged marriages.

B *The romantic idea of love*

Activity

1 Read the following statements about love matches and arranged marriages.

a Which would be made by someone who supports arranged or assisted marriages?

b Which would be made by someone opposed to arranged or assisted marriages?

Explain your choice in each case.

> **i** 'My parents don't understand me; they would not make a good choice.'

> **ii** 'If you don't love someone you should not marry them.'

> **iii** 'I thought he loved me. My Mum told me to get to know him better before I married him. She was right.'

> **iv** 'I want to marry Anne. It's my life and my choice.'

> **v** 'My parents love me and they understand me best. They will find someone really suitable for me.'

> **vi** 'My parents will not choose my partner for me, but they will help me find someone suitable.'

Research activity

Muslims may be helped to find their ideal partner by online matchmakers. See **www.qiran.com** and follow the links on 'Tips on Selecting a Marriage Partner' and 'Marriage: Purpose and Obligation'.

Activity

2 Using the information you have gathered on this topic, create an argument both for and against the claim that arranged marriages are best.

Study tip

When creating an argument for and against something, imagine that two different people are speaking. One is speaking in support of the issue, the other is speaking against. You are writing a script for each one of them to read.

Extension activity

'You get married, then you fall in love.'

'You fall in love, then get married.'

Think about each of these situations. In each case, what do you think your love for your partner could be based on?

Some Muslims see arranged marriages as being simply part of the culture of some Islamic societies rather than part of Islam. They are not unique to Islam; they happen in communities where men and women do not mix freely. Some people believe that an arranged marriage has a better chance of success than one based on falling in love, not least because after an arranged marriage both families will do everything they can to make the relationship work.

Summary

You should now be able to explain that in an arranged or assisted marriage, the parents play an important part in choosing a partner for their son or daughter, but they will not force them to marry against their will. Some Muslims think these are more successful than love matches.

Polygamy

If you fear you shall not be able to deal justly with the orphans, marry two or three or four women of your choice, but if you fear that you will not be able to deal fairly with them, then marry only one.

Qur'an 4:3

Objectives

Consider and explain the practice of polygamy.

The Qur'an allows men to have up to four wives. This is known as **polygamy**. Muslim scholars have debated the exact meaning of this verse in great detail. It was revealed just after the battle of Uhud which left many Muslim widows and fatherless children, and some scholars think that this is the key to its meaning. They believe that polygamy was allowed only so that these women and children could be accepted into new families. They think that this means that it should only be allowed today in similar circumstances.

Key terms

Polygamy: being married to more than one person at once.

A *Would it be better to be one of several wives rather than on your own?*

Discussion activity

1 Imagine a situation in which there were many more women than men.
   a What advantages could polygamy have in such a situation?
   b What disadvantages could polygamy have?

Only men who are certain that they can treat all their wives fairly are allowed to marry more than one wife. That means, among other things, that they must be able to provide the same standard of housing, food and clothing for each wife and treat each one with equal kindness and consideration. The Qur'an says that this is almost impossible, which rules out polygamy for most men.

From a marriage contract

From the husband:

I will not seek sexual pleasure outside marriage.

While I am married to you I will not take another wife except with your permission.

If it is not God's will that I father your children, and if he has made my body in such a way that this is impossible, then I will allow you a divorce.

From the wife:

I will not seek sexual pleasure outside marriage.

If it is not God's will that I bear you children, and if he has made my body in such a way that this is impossible, then you may take another wife.

Activity

1 Read the extract from a marriage contract.
   a Would you allow your husband to have a second wife?
   b Would you allow your wife to divorce you if you could not give her children? Give reasons for your answer.

Most Muslim men have only one wife but there are some circumstances under which it may be better to have more than one. Islam teaches that it is natural for human beings to want both sex and children, and that it would be cruel to deny someone the pleasure of either of them. It also teaches that marriage is the only lawful way sexual desire can be expressed in Islam. Remember both these facts as you tackle Activity 2.

B   *A man who wants a child may benefit from having more than one wife*

Research activity

Polygamy is practised not only within Islam. Read about the experience of one woman who found being one of her husband's eight wives a very positive experience by looking up www.islamfortoday.com/polygamy3.htm

Activity

2   Read the two scenarios given below. Explain why polygamy might be the best option in each of these cases. Can you think of any more situations in which polygamy might be the best choice?

Scenario 1

A man wants to have children, but his wife is unable to have any. His options are: to remain childless; to divorce and remarry; or to take another wife.

Scenario 2

A wife becomes seriously ill and unable to satisfy her husband's sexual desires. His options are: to do without sex; to have sex outside marriage; to divorce and remarry; or to take another wife.

Study tip

You will need to know examples when polygamy could be useful as well as reasons why it may not work.

C   *Could polygamy mean that fewer children grow up lonely?*

Extension activity

Consider why Islam does not allow a woman to have more than one husband.

What advantages and disadvantages do you think there could be for children growing up in a family where their father has more than one wife?

Summary

You should now be able to explain the practice of polygamy, and know that although Muslims believe that God has allowed polygamy, most think it is allowed only under special conditions.

5.6 Sexual relationships outside marriage

Pre-marital sex

Islam forbids **pre-marital sex** and calls it zina or fornication. The Qur'an says that if an unmarried woman or man is found guilty of having sex before marriage, they must be whipped one hundred times.

Beliefs and teachings

Those who fornicate, strike each one with one hundred lashes of the whip. Let not pity for the two hold you back from obedience to God, if you believe in God and the last day. And let a party of believers witness their punishment.

Qur'an 24:2

Anything that could lead to pre-marital sex is also forbidden or strongly discouraged. The Prophet told his followers that if two unmarried people were left together, the devil was also present, tempting them to sin, so free mixing of the sexes is discouraged. Women have to dress modestly so that they are not a temptation for the men. Muslim parents want sex education to make it clear that the only certain way of not getting pregnant is to avoid sex. They also want it to warn of the danger of sexually transmitted infections like HIV/AIDS. They strongly disapprove of anything that encourages sexual relations between young people. In British society, many people choose to live together rather than get married. Islam strongly disapproves of this.

Objectives

Know and understand the Muslim attitude to pre-marital sex and adultery.

Key terms

Pre-marital sex: a sexual relationship which occurs before marriage takes place.

Adultery: sex outside marriage where one or both of the couple are already married to someone else.

Extension activity

Some people like the idea of a trial marriage before starting the real thing. Consider the advantages and disadvantages of a trial marriage. Then write two paragraphs. One should give arguments in favour and the other arguments against a trial marriage.

A *Does free mixing of the sexes encourage sex outside marriage?*

Activity

1 Here are two situations for you to consider, where people are living together. Read the different opinions from some young Muslims.

a Do you agree with their views?

b Do you think what the student is doing is right?

c Do you think what the unmarried man is doing is right?

A: A male Muslim university student is sharing a house with two Muslim boys and two Muslim girls.

Here are some opinions on the student's situation:

This is wrong. He is upsetting his grandparents.

He is learning how to share with others, and how to get on with women. This will be useful when he gets married.

He is facing too much temptation. This is dangerous.

This is OK; his parents trust him to do the right thing.

A: A Muslim man and his partner Helen have chosen to live together rather than get married. They have a young son.

Here are some opinions on the unmarried father's situation:

This is forbidden in Islam.

This is a bad situation for the child.

The wedding is only a formality, it doesn't matter that they haven't had one. His parents would not have let him marry her, she's not a Muslim. What matters is that they love each other.

B *Should couples with children always get married?*

Adultery

According to Muslim belief, if any married person has a sexual relationship with someone other than their wife or husband then they are committing **adultery**. Adultery is seen as something even more serious than pre-marital sex. This is because the person doing it already has a partner who can satisfy their sexual needs and has broken the promise they made at their wedding. They are also showing a total lack of respect for their partner.

Muslims believe that God has forbidden sex outside marriage for very good reasons. They see these relationships leading to many other evils such as diseases, single mothers struggling to bring up children on their own, children who never know who their father was, and who have no security in their family because their mother lives with a series of different men.

Activities

2 Explain what is meant by 'pre-marital sex'.

3 Explain what is meant by adultery.

4 Give two reasons why not allowing pre-marital sex may be a good thing.

5 'Adultery is always wrong.' Why would many Muslims agree with this?

Study tip

You should be able to link Muslim beliefs about sex outside marriage to Muslim beliefs about marriage.

Summary

You should now know and understand the Muslim attitude to pre-marital sex and adultery. Both are forbidden in Islam. Muslims believe that they have been forbidden by God for good reasons.

Attitudes to homosexuality

Islam's teaching about **homosexuality** is based on a story found in the Qur'an. This is the story of the prophet Lot, who criticised the men of his city for their sexual practices:

Beliefs and teachings

You commit an abomination such as no creature ever did before you. You practise your lusts on men in preference to women. Truly you go beyond the limits set by God.

Qur'an 7:80–81

You come to the men and leave the wives your Lord created for you.

Qur'an 26:165

When the people ignored Lot's message, God destroyed the city and everyone in it except Lot and his companions. This event is said to be a sign to the people.

The traditional Muslim view

Many Muslims take this story to mean that God has forbidden male homosexuality, that is, sexual relationships between two men. Some Muslims describe homosexuality as an unnatural condition, a moral disease which is dangerous for the individual and the society. They believe that no one can be a practising homosexual and a Muslim at the same time.

Today some people think that a person can be born a homosexual. If that is so, then it may be seen to be a perfectly natural way of life for some people. Many Muslims do not agree with this. They think that people become homosexual because of the way they are brought up, or because of something that happened to them when they were children. This means that they have learned to be a homosexual and can learn not to be one if they choose.

Case study

Zayan prayed regularly, fasted in Ramadan, did not drink alcohol and gave what he could to charity. He thought of himself as a good Muslim. He had never had a girlfriend, or been attracted to the opposite sex, and by the time he was 21 he realised that he was a homosexual. He was horrified. He knew that the local Imam preached that you couldn't be a Muslim and gay. His parents wanted him to marry and, at first, for their sake, he agreed. The more he thought about his decision the more wrong it felt. If he married he would make his wife miserable and himself miserable, he decided that he should be proud of what God had made him and not pretend to be something he was not.

The Qur'an does not say how homosexuality should be punished. The majority view is that it should receive the same punishment as adultery, but not all the law schools accept this. One hadith seems

Objectives

Consider and explain differing Muslim attitudes to homosexuality.

Key terms

Homosexuality: a sexual relationship with someone of the same sex.

There are no gay Muslims

A *Some Muslims believe no one can be a good Muslim and also be a homosexual*

B *Same sex relationships are forbidden in many Muslim countries*

to say very clearly what the punishment should be. Muhammad is reported to have told his followers to kill both people involved in the act of homosexual sex. Not all Muslims believe that this is a genuine hadith. It is important to note that it is carrying out homosexual sex that is believed to be wrong, not being a homosexual. Islam also indicates that there must be clear evidence that sex has taken place before any accusation is made.

> Homosexuals are born that way. They can be as good and loving as anyone else.

> A married man who has sex with another man should be stoned to death. An unmarried man should be whipped.

 There are differing muslim attitudes to homosexuality

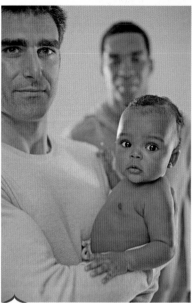

D   *In some countries homosexual couples are allowed to adopt children*

■ An alternative Muslim view

There are homosexuals who consider themselves to be Muslims and many believe that God made them that way. Homosexuality is not illegal in all Muslim countries, and there are Muslim organisations that give support to Muslim homosexuals and Muslim lesbians. However, these groups are strongly opposed by other Muslim groups. Some homosexual Muslims do not consider the Qur'an's teaching on homosexuality to apply today. Others think that God has only forbidden lust and not love. Lust is strong sexual attraction, but love involves caring for each other. They believe that love between a homosexual couple can be as strong and as valuable as love between a mixed sex couple. Some point out that the people that the prophet Lot criticised appear to have been married (he accuses them of leaving their wives). Many homosexuals have never been married. They are not cheating on anyone, so it could be that their relationship with a person of the same sex is not forbidden.

Summary

You should now be able to explain differing Muslim attitudes to homosexuality, and know that these attitudes are divided in Islam. The traditional view is that God has forbidden it and a homosexual act should be punished. Others see it just as another way for people to show their love and care for a partner.

Study tip

Make sure you learn both these points of view Muslims hold on the topic of homosexuality.

Activities

1   'What people do in private should be of no concern of religion.' What do you think? Explain your opinion.

2   'Good Muslims carry out The Five Pillars and support one another. It makes no difference if you are homosexual or not.' What is your opinion?

Attitudes in different Muslim countries

■   Homosexuality is illegal in Saudi Arabia and Iran.

■   Homosexuality is legal in Algeria, Malaysia and Turkey.

5.8 Worship in the home

For Muslims, the home is as much a place of worship as the mosque. Some of the five daily prayers, Qur'an recitation and study, festival celebrations, weddings and the ceremonies linked to childbirth, all take place in the home. Since Muslims also worship God by living their whole life in his service, the Muslim home is also a place of worship simply because this is where Muslims live their Muslim life in obedience to Allah.

Prayer in the home

The pre-dawn and night prayers are usually offered at home because they happen before and after the working day. During the day, women often pray at home rather than in the mosque because they cannot leave the children alone. Ideally, a Muslim home would have a separate room where all the family could pray together. Usually they simply put down prayer mats. The room used for prayer will often show the direction for prayer by putting a picture of the Ka'aba on the wall they must face.

A *Prayers may be offered at home*

Study of the Qur'an

The home is also an important place for Qur'an study and recitation. All Muslims have a lifelong duty to study the Qur'an and to improve their knowledge of God's teaching. Ideally they would study the Qur'an in Arabic, so parents will begin to teach Arabic to their children. The father takes the role of the Imam of the family. He leads both the prayers and the Qur'an study.

The contents and decoration of the home can show that it is a place of worship. Muslims worship God by obeying the rules he has given. Parents are expected to teach their children about Islam and to lead by example so that their children know the right way to behave.

Food is always halal, and family members and visitors are always treated with respect. Within the home, Muslims can live the life they believe God has meant them to live.

Objectives

Describe and explain worship in the home, and consider its significance.

Study tip

It is important to remember that for Muslims worship is much more than just carrying out rituals like prayer.

Research activity

Find out more about the ceremonies linked to the birth of a Muslim child. See www.bbc.co.uk/religion and follow the links to 'Islam' and 'Rites and rituals'.

B *Beautiful copies of the Qur'an may be used at home*

C   *The father may lead the family in Qur'an recitation and study*

D   *Preparing and eating food according to Islamic law is part of worship*

My Muslim home

There are no images of any living things either in pictures or as ornaments, because images can lead to idol worship. Smoking is banned because it is a danger to the smoker and others. On the walls are pictures of mosques around the world, and in the room we use for prayer, qiblah is shown by a picture of a mihrab. There are separate sitting rooms for men and women for when we have visitors. The television will only be turned on for Islamic and educational programmes, because other programmes show non-Muslim behaviour which could lead our children astray.

Case study

Activity

1   Read the description of a Muslim home given in the case study and answer the following questions:

a   Why do Muslim houses not contain images of living things?

b   Why would a Muslim house have extracts from the Qur'an displayed on the walls?

c   How does the passage show that the owner of the house has great respect for those who live in it and visit it?

d   What do you think would be the most obvious difference between the home of a Muslim and a non-Muslim?

e   What type of TV programme do you think a Muslim father would not want his children to watch, and why?

⊂⊃links

For a reminder of what the terms qiblah and mihrab mean, see Chapter 3, pages 60–61.

Activities

2   How important do you think it is for a Muslim to live in a Muslim family?

3   'The home is more important than the mosque as a place of worship.' What is your opinion?

Summary

You should now be able to describe and explain worship in the home, and understand its significance. Prayer and Qur'an study both take place in the home. Living a Muslim life is all about worship, and this is centred on the home.

5.9 The contribution of the mosque to family life

The centre of community life

The mosque is the centre of the local and national Muslim community, and it contributes to family life in many different ways. In some areas of Britain, the mosque provides support and advice to families in the national language of the Muslim communities in its area. This means that those whose English is poor can be helped to do the day-to-day things that they would otherwise find very difficult. It also means that people who might be lonely and isolated in British society have somewhere to meet and socialise. This is very important for those Muslim families who have only been in Britain a short while.

The madrassah

The madrassah is the Islamic school which is often part of the mosque. It teaches Muslim children about their religion by teaching them Arabic and how to recite the Qur'an, how to pray and what to believe. This helps parents to bring up their children as good Muslims. Classes for adults will offer advanced study in the Qur'an and Islamic teaching so that parents learn enough to be able to bring up their children properly.

A *The mosque helps families to carry out their religious duties by teaching Muslim children to pray*

Festivals and pillars

The mosque plays an important part in the way each family celebrates the festivals of Islam and carries out its other religious duties. The mosque sets out the official times for prayer, and for the beginning and end of Ramadan. It provides a meeting place for all the families so that they can celebrate and worship together and become stronger as a community. Without such a centre many families would not get to know the other Muslims in their area. Also, they would not have the moral support that comes from being one of many, all trying to achieve the same goals.

Objectives

Describe and explain the contribution of the mosque to family life, and consider its importance.

links

See Chapter 3 for more information about the mosque.

Extension activity

'A mosque is a centre of worship, but people are going to the mosque for the wrong reasons.' What is your opinion? Consider all the evidence you can find on this page.

B *Mosques are part of the community in many British cities*

Weddings, divorces and funerals

These are important events in family life and the mosque can organise all of them. It may have somewhere large enough for weddings to take place and will, for a fee, provide an Imam to lead the service. The experts in Shari'ah law based at the mosque can grant a woman a divorce from her husband and give rulings on things like child custody and maintenance. When the time comes, the mosque will have a room where the family can prepare the body for burial.

C *Muslim graveyard*

A social centre for young people

Many families worry about what their teenagers do with their time. Many larger mosques provide social clubs and other facilities, like gyms, just for the use of young people. The aim is to keep them off the streets where they could get into trouble, and perhaps to keep them away from non-Muslims, who might be a bad influence. Many non-Muslim teenagers have such a different lifestyle that the Muslim teenagers could be tempted to copy it.

Advice and support

The larger central mosques which are used for Friday community prayers, often have experts available to give information, advice and support on anything to do with Islam. The family could need these people to help settle disputes between parents and children, or between the parents themselves, about the right way to behave. They could also advise on matters such as correct female dress. The law of Islam covers so many aspects of life that Muslim families are often in need of advice.

D *Gym equipment and sports clubs may be provided for young people*

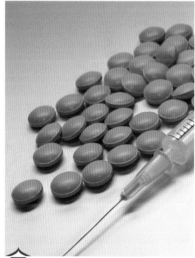

E *The mosque can give advice about the medicines and vaccinations a child may have*

Summary

You should now be able to describe and explain how the mosque contributes to family life, and is of great importance to the family and to the local Muslim community.

Activities

1. How does the mosque support the religious life of a family?

2. How does the mosque support the social life of a family?

3. 'The mosque is more important for Muslim families as a social centre than it is as a religious centre.' What is your opinion? Explain your answer. What do you think?

Study tip

You must be able to recall both the religious and the social work of the mosque, and understand how it contributes to community life.

5

Family life – summary

For the examination, you should be able to:

✔ recall and explain the main parts of the marriage ceremonies and their significance

✔ understand the procedures and arrangements for remarriage and divorce

✔ explain and consider the practice of arranged marriages

✔ explain and consider the practice of polygamy

✔ know and understand Muslim attitudes to sexual relationships outside marriage – pre-marital sex and adultery

✔ know and understand Muslim attitudes to homosexuality

✔ describe and explain worship in the home including prayer and the study of the Qur'an

✔ describe and explain the contribution of the mosque to family life.

Sample answer

1 Write an answer to the following examination question:

'Worship in the home is more important than worship in the mosque.'

Do you agree? Give reasons for your answer, showing that you have thought about more than one point of view.

(6 marks)

2 Read the following sample answer:

> Women and children often worship in the home, because they don't have time to go to the mosque, so for them it is more important. On Fridays, and during the festivals, everyone goes to the mosque. They get together to pray and hear a sermon. The Imam is at the mosque so it is important to go there. I think worship in the mosque is more important than worship in the home.

3 With a partner, discuss the sample answer. It makes several good points, how do you think it could be improved?

4 What mark would you give this answer out of 6? Look at the mark scheme in the Introduction on page 7 (AO2). What are the reasons for the mark you have given?

Practice questions

1 Look at the photograph below and answer the following questions.

(a) Explain what Muslims understand by a marriage contract. *(4 marks)*

(b) Explain what Muslims understand by polygamy. *(4 marks)*

(c) Explain Muslim attitudes to divorce. *(4 marks)*

(d) 'Couples should never live together before they marry.'
Do you agree? Give reasons for your answer, showing that you have thought
about more than one point of view. Refer to Islam in your answer. *(6 marks)*

Study tip You could use arguments from Islam to support the point of view and arguments which
non-Muslims would use to express a different point of view.

(e) 'Arranged marriages are not likely to succeed. They do not give the couple an
opportunity to get to know each other.'
Do you agree? Give reasons for your answer, showing that you have thought
about more than one point of view. Refer to Islam in your answer. *(6 marks)*

Study tip Make sure you think clearly about what Muslims understand by 'arranged marriage' before
you start your answer to this question.

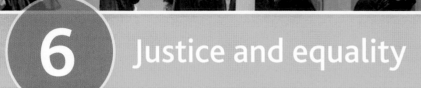

6 Justice and equality

6.1 Introduction

What is justice?

Justice is an ideal that every Muslim aims to achieve. Justice basically means fairness. Muslims believe that justice is one of the supreme values of Islam, and that one of the main purposes of the prophets was to bring justice to the earth. One of the names of God is 'The Just' which in part means 'The One who treats everyone in the way that they have the right to be treated, and the way they deserve'. Every Muslim should try to develop this quality in their life, so that they aim to live in such a way that they are fair to everyone, and make sure that everyone gets what they are entitled to.

God commands that Muslims should treat everyone fairly and show justice even to those they hate. This affects the way that Muslims treat prisoners as well as those who attack Islam.

The opposite of justice is injustice, unfairness and not giving people what they are entitled to. Almost every day there are stories in the news about people who are treated unfairly because of their age, the colour of their skin, their sex and, sometimes, their religion.

Objectives

Understand what is meant by justice and equality and know some key teachings about justice and equality.

Key terms

Justice: bringing about what is right, fair, according to the law or making up for a wrong that has been committed.

Equality: that people should be given the same rights and opportunities regardless of sex, religion, race, etc.

A *Justice is an important ideal in Islam*

Discussion activity

1 Think about examples of unfairness you have come across. In each case give a brief outline of the situation and say why you thought it was unfair. Here are two examples to get you started.

a Two people do the same job but one gets paid more than the other.

b One person is blamed for what someone else has done.

B *Muslims campaigning for justice*

What is equality?

Equality is another ideal that Muslims aim to achieve. It is very closely linked to justice. This is because if you treat people differently for no good reason, you are not treating them as equals and not treating them fairly. Muslims who live their life following the ideal of equality will want to make sure that, as far as possible, everyone has the same opportunities. This would mean that any differences in lifestyle between people would only be the result of their own choices, not because of their race, colour, disability or gender, or any other factor over which they have no control.

Islam is committed to the idea that all people have equal worth, meaning that everyone is as important as everyone else. People are different: some are black, others white; some are male, others female; some are Pakistani and others Arab. Islam teaches that none of these differences means that one group is better than another. People should be judged only according to how well they have lived a life of obedience to God.

Beliefs and teachings

We created you from a single pair of a male and a female, and made you into tribes and nations. Truly the best among you in God's sight is he who is the most righteous.

Qur'an 49:13

For Muslim men and women, for believing men and women, for devout men and women, for true men and women, for men and women who are patient and constant, for men and women who humble themselves, for men and women who give in Charity, for men and women who fast, for men and women who guard their chastity, and for men and women who engage much in Allah's praise, for them has Allah prepared forgiveness and great reward.

Qur'an 33:35

C *Equality of opportunity means all wheelchair users should be able to access all areas*

Study tip

When you are asked to explain an ideal or a concept like 'justice', write down one clear statement to answer the question, then write a second statement to add detail, an explanation, or to provide an example.

Activities

1. Explain what Muslims understand by the ideal of justice.
2. Explain what Muslims understand by the ideal of equality.
3. Explain what Muslims understand by injustice.
4. Write out this paragraph and complete it by choosing the correct words from the following list to put in the gaps:

| India | Women | colour | men | Arab |

Islam teaches that the _____ of your skin does not make you better or worse than other people. _____ are not superior to men, and _____ are not superior to women. God does not judge anyone according to their birth, so being an _____ is not better than being a Pakistani, and being born in England does not make you better than someone born in _____ .

Summary

You should now understand what is meant by justice and equality and know some key teachings about justice and equality. Muslims believe that they are both important.

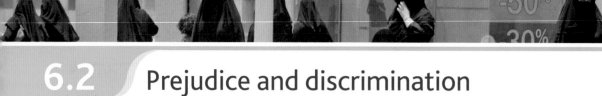

Prejudice and discrimination

What is prejudice?

To be prejudiced is literally to 'pre-judge' someone, so prejudice is a judgement made about people before you have met them; any prejudices you have will affect the way you feel about these people and the way you treat them. You can be prejudiced in someone's favour or prejudiced against them, and prejudice may lead to you treating them unfairly. Prejudices may also be revealed in what we say or write about a group of people or an individual.

Objectives

Know and understand the meaning of the terms prejudice and discrimination.

Key terms

Prejudice: unfairly judging someone before the facts are known.

Discrimination: to act against someone on the basis of sex, race, religion, etc. This is usually a negative action.

Gender: another word for a person's sex.

Activity

1 Identify and discuss the prejudices shown in these statements.
- I've never met a Muslim, but I don't like them.
- When I hear someone speak with a strong accent, I assume that they are stupid.
- I can see from her address that she lives in a posh part of town, so she must be a snob.
- Poor people are lazy.
- Men who only make decisions after consulting their wives are weak.

Each of the statements in Activity 1 expresses a **prejudice**. The speakers have not got any evidence about the people they are drawing a conclusion about. They have formed their opinion before they have met them or got to know what they are like. Such prejudices are often based on stereotypes. Stereotypes are oversimplified views of groups or types of people.

- There are national stereotypes: e.g. All Americans are…………
- There are social stereotypes: e.g. On Saturday nights all white teenagers…………
- There are gender stereotypes: e.g. All women believe that…………

People learn prejudices in many ways. They may copy the way family and friends talk about people, and the way that they treat them. They may pick up false impressions from the way people are presented in magazines and on television.

Islam is opposed to prejudice because it is unreasonable, unjust and intolerant. People who respect others as individuals do not label them according to the group they belong to. They form their opinions after they have met them and got to know them.

What is discrimination?

Discrimination is prejudice in action. When people complain about discrimination they are usually complaining about discrimination *against* someone. However, you can show discrimination in favour of people as well. For example, refusing to interview someone with the surname Khan, because you assume that they are not white, is discriminating against them. Choosing to interview someone with the surname Khan, because you assume that they are black, is discriminating in their favour. Both are unfair and neither is based on knowing anything relevant about the individual at all.

A *No gender discrimination here*

Activity

2 In this activity, you will experience prejudice for yourself.

Ask your teacher to make up different rules for two groups of pupils in your classroom. The rules should be unfair; one group of pupils will be treated much worse than the other. Now divide the class into two groups at random – a red group and a blue group. When everyone knows their group (not before), the teacher will give you your rules. Remember – you don't deserve what you get, just like those who are born male, female, black, white or disabled don't deserve to be sometimes treated unfairly.

a Do the people with the good rules (that they don't deserve) feel happy?

b How do the people with the bad rules feel?

This is prejudice in action.

Prejudice and discrimination today

Some of the most common forms of prejudice and discrimination found in Britain, and many other countries, today are based on race, religion, **gender** and disability. It is not always easy for those who are being discriminated against to know exactly why they are being targeted.

- Racial prejudice: judgements are made about individuals based only on their race.
- Religious prejudice: judgements are made about individuals based only on the religion they follow.
- Gender prejudice: judgements are made based only on whether the person is male or female.
- Disability prejudice: judgements about the person are based only on a single piece of information about them, i.e. they lack an ability which many other people may have.

Activities

3 Explain what is meant by prejudice.

4 Give one example of a statement that expresses a prejudice.

5 Explain what is meant by discrimination.

6 Give one example of behaviour that shows discrimination.

7 Sum up the difference between prejudice and discrimination.

8 Name two types of prejudice and discrimination that can be found in Britain today.

discrimination

[dɪˌskrɪməˈneɪʃən]

1. treatment or consideration of a person based on the group, class, or category to which that person or thing belongs rather than on individual merit
· *racial discrimination*

B *Definition of discrimination*

Research activity

Find out how British laws protect people from discrimination on the basis of race, gender, religion and ability by looking at **www. equalityhumanrights.com** and following the link to 'Your Rights'.

C *Muslims protesting against racial and religions prejudice*

Extension activity

Find out what is meant by Islamophobia and how Islamophobia may be shown.

Summary

You should now know and understand that a prejudice is a judgement made without any evidence being considered, and discrimination is acting on that prejudice.

Study tip

Good examples of prejudice and discrimination will help you to explain them in the examination.

Causes of prejudice and discrimination

There are many reasons why people may be prejudiced against one another.

Ignorance and fear

Prejudice often comes from ignorance. If people do not understand the reasons why others have different skin colour, clothes or accents, or why others have different customs, then they may disrespect them, or even be afraid of them. Ignorance like this also means that people pick up misleading ideas about anyone who is different from themselves, and then accept these ideas without question.

Separation

If groups do not mix in society, there is little chance that they will learn about each other and understand each other. There are separate schools for some groups and people may live separate social lives. Polish people could decide to live together in the same neighbourhood and socialise with those who speak their language, for example. Muslims might also choose to live near other Muslims and not mix in with other people; they may also have their own shops and sometimes not speak English. Similarly, none of this justifies prejudice, but it could explain some of it.

Stereotypes created by the media

If we personally do not know any blacks, Pakistanis, Muslims, Christians, or white British teenagers, then our image of them may come from television, magazines or newspapers. The impression given of these groups may not be accurate or fair. Textbooks could also stereotype different groups of people and so lead to prejudice and discrimination.

Activity

1. Prejudices can show themselves when people make negative judgements about others based on the way they look. Write a short paragraph under the heading 'It is wrong to judge by appearances'.

Attitudes of role models

The way parents, teachers, politicians, television presenters, footballers and other influential people treat people who are different from them, sets the standard for others to follow. If they do not treat other people with respect then nor will the people who follow their example. This is why some prejudices are simply a result of upbringing.

Objectives

Consider the causes of prejudice and be able to explain them.

A *Fear separates people*

B *People may be prejudiced against those who look different from themselves*

Research activity

Find out about different ways in which ethnic minorities and religious groups in Britain are shown in popular television programmes. Do you think that the way they are presented is fair?

The behaviour of a very small minority

The way some people in a particular group behave leads to prejudice against others in that group. Many people will know that the terrorists who killed over 3000 people in New York in America in 2001 called themselves Muslims. They may also hear about a Muslim girl being forced to marry, or being killed by relatives who disapprove of her choice of husband. None of these actions represent Islam as most Muslims understand it, but they create a negative image in the minds of those who know very little about it.

On 7 July 2005, suicide bombers attacked in London, killing 52 people. In the videos they made just before they carried out the attacks, they claimed that they did this for Islam. Research has shown that the attacks had an immediate effect on the way some people felt about Muslims in Britain. They were less happy about having Muslims as neighbours, and felt that Britain was a more dangerous place to live just because there are Muslims living here.

C   *Images like this could stereotype black people*

Discussion activity

Which of the causes of prejudice do you think is the most important, and why?

D   *Children are not born with prejudices. They learn them from other people*

Activities

2   Choose two of the possible causes of prejudice and discrimination mentioned here. Explain in what ways these can cause prejudice.

3   'The behaviour of English girls abroad causes people to be prejudiced against them.' Do you agree? Give reasons for your answer, showing that you have thought about more than one point of view.

Read the Study tip before answering Activity 3.

Study tip

Remember that the statements you will be given to think about in the examination are not always true. They are presented to help you argue from different points of view. You should show that there are different views about the statement and different evidence that can be used to support these views.

Summary

You should now understand that prejudice and discrimination have many different causes, including ignorance, social separation, upbringing, media stereotypes and the behaviour of the community itself.

Britain is traditionally a Christian country, and some non-Christians believe that they are being discriminated against because of their **religion**.

A *Different treatment for Christians and Muslims in Britain*

For Christians	For Muslims
Christmas and Easter are public holidays, so families can get together to celebrate the occasion.	Muslims have to ask for time off school, or take a holiday from work, to celebrate their festivals.
Many Christians can get a Christian education in Church schools paid for by the state.	There are, so far, only a few Muslim schools paid for by the state.
School and work dress codes cause few problems for Christians.	Some school and work dress codes forbid the wearing of the veil.

Each situation has to be carefully examined to see if it is unfair and is a case of discrimination, because it may not be. Rules about dress, for example, may affect everyone and may have a very good reason behind them.

Case study

Bullied for their faith

The anti-bullying campaigners 'Beat Bullying', who surveyed more than 1000 pupils in 2008, found that around 230 thought they had been bullied because of their faith. Ninety said they were bullied because they wore religious symbols.

Adapted from an article by R Garner, www.independent.co.uk, 17 November 2008

Religious prejudice can show itself in many ways, such as name calling, rudeness and lack of consideration. It can be directed at any religious group, for example, towards Christians, Buddhists, Muslims or Jews. It is easier for people to target those whose religion requires them to dress differently. For example, Orthodox Jews, Christian ministers and some Muslims may experience this sort of prejudice. Places of worship and graveyards may also be targeted by vandals who show no respect for the beliefs and feelings of others.

Islam's attitude to other religions

Islam teaches tolerance and understanding between religions. This is one way in which they put justice into action. Justice means giving others the rights that you expect for yourself. Muslims expect others to respect their right to believe and practise their religion, and they give Christians the same rights in return. This is summed up in this verse of the Qur'an:

Beliefs and teachings

I worship not what you worship and you worship not what I worship. To you your religion, to me my religion.

Qur'an 109:1–6

Objectives

Be able to give examples of religious prejudice and discrimination.

Consider Muslim attitudes to other religions.

Key terms

Religion: a set of beliefs, values and practices usually based on the teaching of a spiritual leader.

Discussion activity

1. Do you think the differences between Christians and Muslims listed in Table A mean that British society is unfair to Muslims?

2. Can you think of a job which a Muslim woman might want to do but for which wearing a face-covering veil would be unreasonable?

Extension activity

Consider the advantages and disadvantages of separate schools for separate religions in the UK.

B *Muslims who wear distinctive clothing may be discriminated against*

Shop assistants wanted, Muslims only

Care assistants required – no Jews need apply

Footballer needed for college team. Muslim preferred

D *Christian ministers can be recognised by their clothing and may be discriminated against*

 Applying religious discrimination

The Qur'an instructs Muslims not to insult the gods other people worship, because that would simply lead them to insult Allah and cause hatred between religions.

Beliefs and teachings

Revile not those unto whom they pray beside Allah, lest they wrongfully revile Allah through ignorance.

Qur'an 6:109

God gives people the choice to believe or disbelieve.

Beliefs and teachings

Whoever will, let him believe. Whoever will, let him disbelieve.

Qur'an 18:30

The Qur'an forbids anyone to force their religion on one another.

Beliefs and teachings

There is no compulsion in religion.

Qur'an 2:256

The Qur'an shows particular respect to the Christian and Jewish religions, even though it criticises some of their beliefs. It mentions mosques, churches and Jewish synagogues as places where: 'the name of God is remembered in great measure'. It also allows believers to defend them against attack if necessary. When Muhammad set up the Muslim community in Madinah, he gave religious freedom to the Jews in the city, and many Muslims take this as the model they should follow today.

Summary

You should now be able to give examples of religious prejudice and discrimination, and know that it can take many forms. You should also be aware of Muslim attitudes to other religions, and that Islam teaches tolerance and respect for the beliefs and views of others.

Study tip

Short quotations from the Qur'an can be very useful in your answers.

Research activity

Understanding between religions can be built up by what is sometimes referred to as 'interfaith dialogue'. Find out how religions are trying to work together and build up understanding between them by looking up www.interfaith.org.uk and following the link to 'Local Inter Faith Zone'.

Activities

1 Give **two** ways in which prejudice may be shown against religious believers.

2 Give **one** verse from the Qur'an which suggests that everyone has a right to believe what they choose.

3 'Everyone should show respect for the views of others, but that does not mean that you agree with their views.' What do you think an Imam might say about this?

Race and disability discrimination

Race discrimination

Some people in Britain do feel that they are discriminated against because of the colour of their skin. They do not trust other people not to be racist. They may suspect that they are being treated unfairly because of their **race**, whenever they are not offered a job they have applied for, or have not been chosen to play in a team, or have not been given a pay rise. They may be right but they may be wrong. It is not always easy to tell when discrimination has really happened, whether someone has been disadvantaged because of their skin colour, religion or disability; or whether there may be some ordinary and fair reason why these seemingly unfair things have happened.

It is good for people to be made to laugh at themselves.

Racist jokes are an insult to the race that is being made fun of.

 Are racist jokes an acceptance type of humour?

Muslim attitudes to different races

Islam is 'colour blind', which means that it takes no notice of people's colour or race when it judges how good or bad someone is. Muslims expect everyone to be treated with equal respect. The Qur'an calls the variations in languages and colours among the people of the earth signs from God which show his greatness and his power, so no colour or race is any better than another. This was summed up by the Prophet during his farewell sermon:

> 66 *Oh people, truly your Lord and Sustainer is One and your ancestor is one. All of you descend from Adam and Adam was made of earth. There is no superiority for an Arab over a non-Arab, nor for a non-Arab over an Arab; neither for a white man over a black man nor a black man over a white man except for superiority gained through God consciousness (taqwah). Indeed the noblest amongst you is the one who is most deeply conscious of God.* 99
>
> *Adapted from Islam the Natural Way, A W Hamid (1989)*

Objectives

Be able to give examples of racial prejudice and discrimination.

Consider Muslim attitudes to different races and abilities.

Key terms

Race: a group of people with the same ethnic background.

Study tip

Make sure that you can give examples of racial prejudice in action.

B *A job applicant. The fact that she is black should be irrelevant*

∞links

See Chapter 2, pages 48–49, to see how the hajj reveals the international brotherhood of Islam.

C   *Children are not racist. Prejudice is taught to them by their parents and by society*

Attitudes to disability

According to Islam, all human beings are born in the condition that God has planned for them; some are able bodied, some are not. It is the duty of every Muslim to accept the condition God has given to them, and to serve him in any way they can. This means that someone born disabled is not worse than anyone else, just different. They are entitled to the same respect and rights as everyone else and, as far as possible, to the same opportunities.

Disability discrimination

Case study

Not all Muslims live up to this ideal. Parents looking for marriage partners for their son or daughter can be unwilling to choose a disabled partner. There are various examples on the internet of young disabled Muslims, or Muslims with lifelong medical conditions, who have heard relatives say, 'Nobody will want to marry her now.'

Activity

Copy this paragraph into your notes. Each of the following words or phrases fits into one of the gaps in the sentences below:

opportunities   service to God   international

respect   racial discrimination   hajj

When a person is treated unfairly because of the colour of their skin, or the country they come from, this is an example of _____ .

Islam teaches that the only thing that makes one person better than another is their _____ .

The community of Islam is an_____ community. This is clearly illustrated in the _____ .

Muslims should treat all people with _____ and work to make sure that everyone has equal _____ .

Extension activity

'All races are equal in Islam.' Write a magazine article using this as its title. You may want to refer to the hajj to illustrate the article.

Not all Muslims are committed to racial equality. The Muslim author and human rights activist Irshad Manji makes the case that Arab racism runs deep. As one ilustration, Professor Manji records that at a public meeting she heard an Arab Muslim shout:

> 66 *Pakistanis are not real Muslims. They are converts. Islam was revealed to the Arabs.* 99
>
> *The Trouble with Islam: A Wake-up Call for Honestly and Change, I Manji (2005)*

D   *A talented wheelchair athlete*

Summary

You should now be able to give examples of racial prejudice and discrimination, and understand that they can take many forms. You should also be aware of Muslim attitudes to different races and abilities. Islam teaches racial equality.

The role of women in Islam

Beliefs and teachings

The believing men and women, are associates and helpers of each other. They work together to promote all that is beneficial and discourage all that is evil.

Qur'an 9:71

Objectives

Consider the role and importance of women in Islam.

The woman as wife and mother

Many Muslims believe that the most important role for a woman is her role as wife and mother. This is seen as the role for which God created women and as their natural role, because only they can give birth. This role is so important that the woman is allowed to put the needs of her body and her children first, and is excused duties which men are expected to perform. For example, when she is pregnant, or during her period, a woman does not have to fast or pray. When she is busy looking after her children, she does not have to go to the mosque.

The role of mother is given a very high status in Islam. In non-Muslim societies like Britain, being a mother is not always seen as a high status role. However, in Islam it is considered so important that mothers are said to be the people most worthy of love and respect. Mothers are described as a gift from God, and children are taught that they should give their mothers a lifetime of love and care.

Research activity

1 Find out more about women at the time of the Prophet by using web pages such as www.pbs.org/muhammad/ma_women.shtml

2 Find out about the role of one famous professional Muslim woman in Britain today. Use the Muslim Women Power List at www.thelist2009.com

A *Is this a woman's most important role?*

B *A Muslim businesswoman*

Responsibilities

It is the mother's responsibility to run a Muslim home and to bring up the next generation of Muslims. She is expected to teach her children the basics of their religion. This includes teaching them how to pray and how to recite some of the Qur'an, and making sure that prayer and other Muslim duties, like fasting, are carried out properly. She is responsible for making sure her children are educated and learn the manners and customs of Islam. She is also responsible for making sure that they are prepared for their own roles as husband and father or wife and mother.

Beliefs and teachings

Paradise lies at the feet of a mother.   *Hadith*

links

See pages 136–137 for more on the status of women

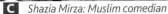

C   *Shazia Mirza: Muslim comedian*

D   *Shirin Ebadi: Iranian human rights activist, feminist and human rights lawyer*

Women at the time of the Prophet

At the time of the Prophet, many women had roles outside the family. Khadijah, wife of the Prophet, ran a successful trading business. There were women farmers, leatherworkers, Imams, scholars, warriors and medics. They played a full part in the life of the community. Today, in many countries including Britain, many Muslim women work in professional roles such as lawyers, teachers and doctors, as well as in a range of other jobs. They do this with the support of their husbands and families.

E   *Wearing modest dress does not have to limit a Muslim woman to working in the home*

Activities

1   What is said to be the most important role for a Muslim woman?

2   Why is it an important role?

3   What other roles may a Muslim woman have? Give **three** examples.

4   'Muslim women can do any job a man can do.' Do you agree? Explain your answer.

Summary

You should now understand the role and importance of women in Islam. The role of a wife and mother in Islam is given a very high status but women are also allowed to work outside the home.

Study tip

Always support your point of view with reasons or evidence.

6.7 Women's rights

Beliefs and teachings

And women shall have rights similar to the rights against them, according to what is fair, but men have a degree over them.

Qur'an 2:228

Objectives

Summarise the rights of women in Islam.

Consider Muslim attitudes to women.

Property

All Muslim women have the right to be treated with fairness and respect. They have the right to be supported by men and to receive an education. When they marry, their property remains their own. They have the right to spend their money, and their dowry or marriage payment, in any way they like. Men do not have this right; they have to spend their money on supporting the family. Women have different rights from men in other areas as well. Sometimes it may appear that Muslim women have fewer rights and are treated unfairly compared to men.

Case study

Women in Saudi Arabia

In Saudi Arabia men and women live separate lives. Saudi women are not allowed to drive. They must not leave the house without a chaperone, or be on their own with an unrelated male. They may only work with permission from their father, husband or nearest male relative. When they appear in public, they must wear a black gown and head covering, so that only their face and hands may be seen. When they are in restaurants and cafes, they eat in special family sections, which are screened off from those used by single men. They attend girls-only schools and university departments. There are female-only gyms and shops and, in the capital city, Riyadh, there is even a female-only shopping mall.

Activity

1 Read the Case study carefully. Write out the following sentences adding information from the case study to fill in the gaps.

a Women in Saudi Arabia do not always have the right to work. They can work if……………………

b Men and women are separated in Saudi Arabia in many ways. Some of these are……………………

links

See Chapter 4, pages 88–89, for more information about Islamic dress.

A *Shopping in Riyadh, Saudi Arabia*

links

More information on women's rights in Islam can be found at **www.pbs.org/wgbh/globalconnections/mideast/questions/women/index.html**

Inheritance

Beliefs and teachings

God gives you these commands about your children's inheritance: to the male, a portion equal to that of two females: if only daughters, two or more, their share is two-thirds of the inheritance; if only one, her share is a half.

Qur'an 4:11

When parents die, a son is entitled to twice as much as his sister. This seems unfair, but some Muslims believe it makes total sense when you consider that women are not expected to support themselves. A man is expected to provide housing, food and clothing for his wife and family. This is how much of his inheritance will be spent. Women may spend their share on whatever they please; it is not their duty to spend it on others.

Polygamy

Men are allowed up to four wives, according to the Qur'an, but women may have only one husband. Some Muslims believe that it could be to women's advantage to allow men to marry more than one wife. This is because, if there were not enough men to go round, it would mean that every woman could have a sexual partner and possibly a child.

Divorce

A man may divorce his wife but a wife has to ask a court to give her a divorce. Some non-Muslims see this as one of the main ways in which Islam is unfair to women. Muslims argue that involving the Muslim authorities is a way of making sure that the woman gets the maintenance she and her children are entitled to. They see the custom as a way of protecting women.

Extension activity

'Islam is unfair to men.' Write a speech to support this idea. The purpose of the speech is to convince a group of Muslim women that they should do more to support their husbands.

B   *Women entering Cairo mosque through women only entrance*

⚭links

See Chapter 5, pages 108–109 for more information about polygamy.

See Chapter 5, pages 104–105 for more information on Divorce.

Activity

2 a Go through each of the four rights mentioned in this section: property, inheritance, marriage and divorce. Write down the rights of men on the left-hand side of the page and the rights of women on the right-hand side, so that you can see the differences between them very clearly.

   b Give two reasons why some people might say that Islam is unfair to women. Support your statements with evidence.

Summary

You should now know the rights of women in Islam, and understand Muslim attitudes to women. Women have different rights from men in Islam, but many Muslims believe that there are good reasons for these differences.

Study tip

Remember that you will need to be able to consider topics like this from different points of view.

Men and women

There are many different views in Islam about the relationship between men and women. The discussions often centre on the exact meaning of some important verses in the Qur'an. One such verse is Surah 4 verse 34. Two different versions of parts of this verse, both based on accepted English translations of the Qur'an, are given here. Each one interprets the Arabic words of the Qur'an in a different way. They illustrate two of the different understandings of the relationship between men and women found in Islam.

Version A

Men are in charge of women because God has made one of them excel the other.

Summary based on the translation by M Pickthall

Version B

Men are the protectors and maintainers of women because God has given one more strength than the other.

Summary based on the translation by Yusuf Ali

It is easy to see from version A why some non-Muslims quote this verse as proof that women do not have equality with men in Islam. From version B it is easy to see why others believe that women have a special status in Islam, and that it is the duty of men to provide for them.

Activities

1   How does version A describe the relationship between men and women?
2   How does version B describe the relationship between men and women?

Obedient women

The next part of the verse, in both translations, states that good women are obedient. Some Muslims believe that this means a wife must obey her husband, but that he can only command her to do what God would also command. Some think that a woman should obey her husband in all things. They think that she would be disobeying her husband if she left the house without his permission, spoke to him impolitely, or did the opposite of what he liked. This would clearly give the woman a lower status than the man, and it follows on from the idea that men are in charge of women. Other Muslims do not believe that the verse is about obeying husbands. They think that it simply reminds Muslims that women, and men, must be obedient to God.

The meaning of the last part of the verse is debated most strongly. It tells a man what to do if he fears that the woman will not obey. First he is told to criticise her, then, if that fails to solve the problem, to refuse to sleep with her. The last instruction is usually translated 'beat

A *The symbol for Islamic feminism*

her'. Some Muslims believe that this translation shows a complete misunderstanding of the meaning of the Arabic words. They believe that the true meaning is that the husband of a disobedient wife should, as a last resort, 'strike her out of the marriage' which means, divorce her.

Research activity

2 Find out more about how some Muslims understand this verse, and their view of the role and status of women in Islam, by using **www.submission.org**. Follow the link 'Women in Islam' then the link 'Misconceptions about the women in Islam'.

These examples show that there are great differences between Muslims in the way that they understand the relationship between men and women in Islam. Some Muslim feminists believe that men have deliberately picked the meaning of the words which favour them above women. Some Muslim men believe that the women are deliberately changing the meaning of the words to suit themselves.

Extension activity

Qur'an 4:34 can be interpreted in a way that favours men and a way that favours women.

Imagine two Muslim speakers summing up this verse as they understand it. One supports a pro-male interpretation; the other favours a pro-female interpretation. What would each one say?

Muslim career women

In some Muslim countries, women need the permission of their nearest male relative before they can study or work. In many cases permission is given, and the women go on to have successful careers in many areas of life. A recent survey of Pakistani and Bangladeshi Muslim women in Britain found that many had the same ambition as non-Muslim women: to combine a career with having a family. It also found that their husbands generally supported their ambitions. In March 2009, a Muslim Women Power List was published as a celebration of successful Muslim women in Britain, and many of them had the support and encouragement of their husbands.

Research activity

3 Find out more about Qur'an 4:34 and how this verse has been interpreted in different ways. Read the whole of the verse and try to compare different versions.

Activity

3 'A good woman should obey her husband.' What do some Muslims understand this to mean?

Case study

Mishal Husain

Mishal Husain is a BBC news and current affairs presenter. She was born in the UK and studied law at Cambridge University. In 2004 she was named 'Young achiever of the year' at the Asian Women of Achievement Awards.

B *Mishal Husain*

∞ links

To find out about the Muslim Women Power List, go to: **www.thelist2009.com**

Summary

You should now understand that different interpretations of Qur'an 4:34 show very different views of the relationship between men and women in Islam.

The status of women

Beliefs and teachings

The believing men and women, are associates and helpers of each other. They work together to promote all that is beneficial and discourage all that is evil.

Qur'an 9:71

Objectives

Consider different views of the status of women in Islam.

We have already seen that the role of the woman as a wife and mother has a very high status in Islam. We have also seen that in some societies, like Saudi Arabia, women are provided with separate facilities to protect them from the attention of men. This section looks at different views about women's status in Islam.

Men and women have equal worth

The Qur'an describes men and women as partners who support each other in carrying out God's work. Many Muslims believe that this means women and men have equal worth. They have different roles. However, both roles are equally important and both are judged only according to how well they have followed God's commands. In the family the different roles of the husband and wife are based on the clear differences between men and women. The husband has to provide for the family, while the wife has children and brings them up as good Muslims. She is the 'queen of the house' (Hadith). Only by working together can the couple make sure that Islam passes on to the next generation, so both are equally important.

A *A woman's lifestyle may depend on the country she is from*

The woman has the better position

Some Muslims believe that the woman's position in the family is better than the man's. This is because she does not have to work and her husband has to provide her with everything she needs.

B *A professional Muslim woman*

Activities

1   Write out the following and fill in the gaps from the information you have now gained.

Islam gives different roles to men and women:

a   One role for a woman is

_____ .

b   One role for a man is

_____ .

2   Explain the idea that men and women have equal worth in Islam.

3   Looking back over all the information you have been given about women in Islam, write a paragraph under the heading 'It is the duty of Muslim men to support and protect women.'

The husband has more responsibility

A husband has to treat his wife with respect. He does have overall authority in the family but, according to many Muslims, this only means that when the couple cannot agree he has to make the final decision. Many Muslim men say that this gives them responsibility rather than power. Some Muslim societies do give men much more authority over women than this and expect women to obey them in all things.

C *Afghan women wearing a burqa*

Both men and women are rewarded for their good actions

> **Beliefs and teachings**
>
> Whoever works righteousness, man or woman, and has faith, to them we will give a new life, a life that is good and pure, and we will give them reward according to the best of their actions.
>
> *Qur'an* 16:97

Conclusions

Muslims believe in gender equality according to law. In other words, both men and women have the right to receive everything that the law of God entitles them to. Both will be judged by God and rewarded for all the good they have done. They also have equal worth, because Islam cannot survive without both sexes carrying out their duty. In the family, men and women have very different roles because the two sexes are very different. These different roles are reflected in the different rights and responsibilities given to men and women. In practice, the way that the role of women is interpreted in different Muslim societies means that women are not always given equal opportunities to men.

Afghanistan under the Taliban

When the militant Muslim group called the Taliban took over Afghanistan between 1996 and 2001 CE, they enforced a very strict law. They closed the girls' schools and the women's hospitals, and they stopped women from working. They forced women to wear clothing, called a burqa, which showed no part of their body and hid their shape. Even their eyes had to be covered by a thin cloth. The women could see through this, but they could not be seen. If a woman broke the law, for example, if her ankle showed beneath her burqa, she would be beaten or whipped.

∞ links

You can look up the term 'burqa' in the Glossary at the back of the book.

Extension activity

Explore the portrayal of the lives of Muslim women in Afghanistan in works of fiction like 'A thousand splendid suns' by Khaled Hosseini.

Study tip

In the examination you will be expected to know about more than one point of view concerning the status of women in Islam.

Summary

You should now know and understand different views of the status of women in Islam. Many believe that a woman has equal worth to a man, but because she is different from a man, she should be treated differently and have different rights.

6

Justice and equality – summary

For the examination, you should be able to:

✓ understand what is meant by justice and equality

✓ know Muslim teaching about and views on justice and equality

✓ understand what is meant by prejudice and discrimination, and know the main types of prejudice, including race, religion and gender

✓ explain causes of prejudice and discrimination

✓ understand Muslim attitudes to prejudice and discrimination

✓ understand the role and status of women in Islam

✓ consider the concept of equal worth as applied to men and women.

Sample answer

1 Write an answer to the following examination question:

Explain Muslim teaching about the role of women.

(6 marks)

2 Read the following sample answer:

> The main role for a woman in Islam is as a wife and mother. This is something only she can do. She runs the family and is the 'queen' of the house. A woman may be allowed to go out to work if her husband allows her to. Women have equal worth to men in Islam because the job they do is very important.

3 With a partner, discuss the sample answer. Some parts of the answer need more detail. How could it be improved?

4 What mark would you give this answer out of 6? Look at the mark scheme in the Introduction on page 7 (AO1). What are the reasons for the mark you have given?

Practice questions

1   Look at the illustration below and answer the following questions.

> Both men and women have very important roles in Islam.

> Women are made to wear the hijab. It's not fair.

> Women are different from men and need to be treated differently.

(a) Explain **two** reasons why people of one religion may be prejudiced against people of a different religion. *(4 marks)*

> **Study tip**   Notice that this question is worth 4 marks even though you are asked for only two reasons. You will have to develop each reason a little, with some detail or an example, to score 4 marks.

(b) 'Women should be treated differently from men.'
What do you think? Explain your opinion. Refer to Islam in your answer. *(3 marks)*

> **Study tip**   Focus on the statement you are being asked to think about. To help you decide what you think about it, write down what it means.
>
> 'Women should be treated differently' means they should not be treated the same as men. Do you agree?

(c) 'Wearing special dress is an important part of being a Muslim woman.'
Do you agree? Give reasons for your answer, showing that you have thought about more than one point of view. *(6 marks)*

> **Study tip**   Aim to write around half a page for a 6-mark question.

(d) Explain what Islam teaches about racial equality. *(6 marks)*

Glossary

A

Abraham: an important prophet of God. Known to Muslims as Ibrahim.

Adhan: the call to prayer.

Adultery: sex outside marriage where one or both of the couple are already married to someone else.

Akhirah: everlasting life after death.

Allah: the Islamic name for God.

Ansar: name given to the early Muslims of Madinah.

Arafat: a plain near to Makkah where pilgrims gather to worship, pray and ask for forgiveness. This takes place on the ninth day of the Islamic month Dhul Hijja, the day before Eid ul Adha.

Arranged marriage: a marriage for which parents will take a leading role in choosing a marriage partner for their son or daughter.

Asr: name for the afternoon prayer time.

Authority: power to give orders to others and expect obedience.

B

Barzakh: the barrier between this world and paradise/hell – a state of waiting after death.

Bismillah: the name for the phrase 'In the name of God the merciful and the compassionate'. The phrase begins most surahs in the Qur'an and is used in daily prayers.

Burqa: outer clothing worn by women to cover the entire body.

C

Compilation: a gathering together into one book of material from more than one source.

Customs: accepted or habitual practices usually of long standing.

D

Day of Judgement: the day when Allah will decide about individual deeds, good and bad, and on reward and punishment.

Discrimination: to act against someone on the basis of sex, race, religion, etc. This is usually a negative action.

Divorce: legal ending of a marriage.

Dowry: a gift made by the man to his bride or to her parents.

Du'a: personal prayer.

E

Eid ul Adha: celebration of the prophet Ibrahim's willingness to sacrifice his son for Allah. Ends the period of hajj.

Eid ul Fitr: celebration of the end of fasting after Ramadan.

Equality: that people should be given the same rights and opportunities regardless of sex, religion, race, etc.

F

Fajr: name for the prayer time just before sunrise.

The Five Pillars of Islam: the five most important duties: to believe, to pray, to give to charity, to fast and to go on pilgrimage.

G

Gender: another word for a person's sex.

H

Hadith: sayings of the Prophet Muhammad. A major source of Islamic law.

Hafiz: person who has learned Qur'an by heart.

Hajj: the annual pilgrimage to Makkah, which all Muslims must undertake at least once in their lives, unless prevented by problems over wealth or health. The fifth pillar of Islam.

Halal: any action or thing which is permitted or lawful.

Haram: any action or thing which is forbidden.

Hell: eternal separation from Allah.

Hijab: modest dress for women – often used to mean the veil or headscarf Muslim women wear – means 'cover'.

Hijrah: the emigration of the Prophet Muhammad from Makkah to Madinah in 622 CE; the Muslim calendar commences from this event.

Homosexuality: a sexual relationship with someone of the same sex.

I

Ihram: special white clothing worn by male pilgrims; the state of holiness entered into when Muslims are performing hajj symbolised by the clothing.

Imam: a person who leads communal prayer; in Shi'ah, the title of Ali and his successors.

Inshallah: the phrase 'God willing', used by Muslims when they promise to do something.

Isha: name for the prayer time at night.

Islam: the name of the religion followed by Muslims; to surrender to the will of God; peace.

J

Jamarat: the name of the three stone pillars at Mina representing evil or temptation.

Jibril: Islamic name for the angel Gabriel.

Jumuah: weekly communal salah performed after midday on a Friday.

Justice: bringing about what is right, fair, according to the law or making up for a wrong that has been committed.

K

Ka'aba: the black covered cube-shaped building in the centre of the Grand Mosque in Makkah.

L

Lifestyle: way of life.

M

Madinah (Medina): Muhammad travelled to Madinah from Makkah in 622 CE. It is regarded as the second holiest city in Islam and is the burial place of Muhammad.

Madrassah: a Muslim school attached to a mosque where young Muslims study Islam.

Maghrib: name for the prayer time at sunset.

Makkah (Mecca): the city where Muhammad was born. The spiritual centre of Islam; it is in Saudi Arabia.

Marriage: a legal union between a man and a woman.

Masjid: the mosque.

Mihrab: a niche indicating the direction of Makkah.

Mina: place to be visited on hajj – stoning of pillars.

Minaret: a tower from which the call to prayer is given.

Minbar: a pulpit for giving Friday sermons.

Modesty: unpretentious manner or appearance.

Mosque: a Muslim place of worship.

Mu'adhin (muezzin): the Islamic call to prayer (the person who calls).

Muhammad: the last and greatest of the prophets of Allah. The name Muhammad means 'praised'.

Muslim: one who has submitted to the will of Allah and has accepted Islam.

Muzdalifah: place where pilgrims hold a night prayer and rest during hajj, after the Stand on Mount Arafat.

P

Paradise: place of perfect happiness; the afterlife.

Pilgrimage: a journey made for religious reasons.

Polygamy: being married to more than one person at once.

Prejudice: unfairly judging someone before the facts are known.

Pre-marital sex: a sexual relationship which occurs before marriage takes place.

the Prophet: title often used for Muhammad, the last of the prophets.

Prophethood: channel of communication with God (risalah).

Prostration: an act of lying with the face downwards in submission to God.

Purdah: an Urdu word often used to describe complete seclusion. Women covering their face and hands when in public.

Q

Qiblah: the direction of Makkah.

Qur'an: the Holy Book revealed to the Prophet Muhammad by the angel Jibril. Allah's final revelation to mankind.

R

Race: a group of people with the same ethnic background.

Rak'ah: a sequence of movements in ritual prayer.

Ramadan: month during which fasting from dawn to sunset is demanded (ninth month of the Islamic calendar).

Recitation: a repeating of a passage or poem from memory.

Religion: a set of beliefs, values and practices usually based on the teaching of a spiritual leader.

Remarriage: when people who have been married before marry again.

Revelation: the words of the Qur'an being shown to Muhammad; Allah shows himself to believers.

Risalah: prophethood; channel of communication.

Ritual: a religious ceremony or series of actions often with symbolic meaning.

S

Sadaqah: good actions or voluntary payments undertaken for charitable reasons.

Salah: prayer with and worship of Allah, performed under the conditions set by the Prophet Muhammad. The second pillar of Islam.

Sawm: fasting from dawn to dusk during Ramadan; sex and smoking are banned when the believer is engaged in this. The fourth pillar of Islam.

Shahadah: Muslim declaration of faith. The first pillar of Islam.

Shari'ah: Islamic law based directly upon the Qur'an and sunnah.

Shi'ah (Shi'i): Muslims who believe in the Imamah, successorship of Ali.

Sunnah: the teachings and deeds of Muhammad.

Sunni: Muslims who believe in the successorship of Abu Bakr, Umar, Uthman and Ali.

Surah: division of the Qur'an. There are 114 in all.

T

Tawhid: oneness and unity of Allah.

U

Ummah: all Muslims are regarded as part of a brotherhood; the nation of Islam.

W

Wahy: the revelation of the Qur'an to Mohammad by a process of inspiration.

Wudu: ritual washing before prayer.

Wuquf: the Stand on Mount Arafat.

Y

Yathrib: former name for Madinah.

Z

Zakah: purification of wealth by giving to the poor; an act of obligatory worship for Muslims.

Zamzam: name of well situated near the Ka'aba.

Zuhr: name for the prayer time just after midday.

Index

Key terms are in blue bold